Visualizing the Blues Tour Schedule

Year	Dates	Venue
2000		
	Oct. 8- Jan 7, 2001	The Dixon Gallery and Gardens Memphis, TN
2001		
	Apr. 29 - Jul. 8	The Ogden Museum of Southern Art, New Orleans, LA
	Oct. 12-Dec. 23	Museum of Contemporary Art, Boulder, CO.
2002		
	Jan. 18 - Mar. 24	Austin Museum of Art Austin, TX
	Apr. 6 - May 26	Columbia Museum of Art Columbia, SC
	Jun. 2-Sept. 8	The Hyde Collection Glens Falls, NY
	Sept. 24-Nov. 24	Telfair Museum of Art Savannah, GA
2003		
	Jan.18-Mar. 23	Georgia Museum of Art Athens, GA

Published as a complement to the exhibition
Visualizing the Blues: Images of the American South, 1862-1999

Organized and circulated by The Dixon Gallery and Gardens
Memphis ,TN

Cover: William Eggleston, *Untitled*, c. 1965
Silver gelatin black and white
Courtesy of the Eggleston Artistic Trust

Editor: Wendy McDaris
Book Design: Calvin Foster / bleuhaus design
Technical Editors: Vivian Kung-Haga and Neil O'Brien
Catalog photography: Pete Ceren
Color Separations: All Systems Colour
Printed in Canada

ISBN 0-945064-04-7 (hc)

photographers

Bob Adelman	William Eggleston	Allison Nowlin
William Albert Allard	Alfred Eisenstaedt	Gordon Parks
George Barnard	Walker Evans	P.H. Polk
E. J. Bellocq	Huger Foote	Jonathan Postal
Margaret Bourke-White	Lee Friedlander	Tom Rankin
Mathew Brady	Alexander Gardner	Arthur Rothstein
Lindsay Brice	William Greiner	Peter Sekaer
Paul Buchanan	Whit Griffin	Andres Serrano
Jane Rule Burdine	Lewis Wickes Hine	Mike Smith
Debbie Fleming Caffery	Birney Imes	W. Eugene Smith
Patty Carroll	Dorothea Lange	Jack Spencer
Henri Cartier-Bresson	Clarence John Laughlin	Mark Steinmetz
Tseng Kwong Chi	David Julian Leonard	Guenevere Taft
William Christenberry	C. C. Lockwood	Doris Ulmann
Maude Schuyler Clay	Deborah Luster	Jeane Umbreit
Florestine Perrault Collins	Danny Lyon	James Perry Walker
Ralston Crawford	Sally Mann	Eudora Welty
Jack Delano	Larry E. McPherson	Edward Weston
Alain Desvergnes	Ashley T. Mitchell	Ernest Withers
Mike Disfarmer	Milly Moorhead	Marion Post Wolcott
Jim Dow	Nicholas Nixon	Logan Young

visualizing the blues

images of the

of the

AMERICAN South

edited by Wendy McDaris
foreward by John Grisham

peter sekaer (1901-1950), *Zulu Parade, Float with Maskers, c.* 1939

acknowledgments

wendy mcdaris

In 1994, I became aware of numbers of photographers who found the South a rich source of inspiration for their work that in turn inspired me to create an exhibition. In the early stages of development, it was clear that a single exhibition could not physically accommodate the vast amount of brilliant images that captured Southern culture from the beginnings of photographic history onward. Instead, *Visualizing the Blues* was conceived as both an evocation of a beloved culture and a body of artistic evidence that bespeaks the multiple powers of the medium of photography. I am indebted to Jay Kamm, Director, The Dixon Gallery and Gardens, for his support of the exhibition, and determination and vision in bringing it to life with the cooperation of the greater Memphis community. Sally Kee, Executive Assistant to Mr. Kamm, has lent much needed advice for which I am thankful.

I wish to extend my deep appreciation to my associate, Anne Ellegood, Assistant Curator, New Museum of Contemporary Art, New York, for the professionalism, diligence, insight, and imagination she brought to curatorial research. Assisting her were Neil O'Brien, Registrar, Vivian Kung-Haga, Assistant Curator, both of the Dixon, to whom I remain indebted for their work on the exhibition's production and installation as well as the catalogue. Jane Faquin, the Dixon's Curator of Education, provided excellent educational outreach programming to augment the exhibition, and James Starks, the Dixon's Preparator, is also to be commended for exceptional attention to the installation of the exhibition. Besides the enthusiastic support of the museum staff, an exhibition of this size could not have been realized were it not for the support of the of the Dixon's Board of Trustees, especially Jack Blair, Allen Morgan, and Herbert Rhea.

Helpful advice, thoughtful opinions, and fresh insights were generously offered by John Lawrence at The Historic New Orleans Collection, Grady Turner and Robert Engel at The New-York Historical Society, Jayne H. Baum, Joel Bernsen, Manuel Borja-Villel, Alain Desvergnes, Debbie de la Houssaye, Vicki Goldberg, J. Richard Gruber, Peter Guralnick, Doreet Harten, Jurgen Harten, Marlene Ivey, Tony Jones, James O. Patterson, Francois Quintin, Carole Sartain, Alistair Smith, Sally Stevens, and Matthew Sweeney.

Without the assistance of galleries, museums, dealers, and collectors many of the works needed to underscore the theme of the exhibition would not have been found. I am most grateful for the kind assistance of Arthé Anthony, William Bearden, Bonni Benrubi, Claire Bertrand, Janet Borden, Melissa Brown, Ann Cain, Belena Chapp, James Conlin, Paula Cooper, Winston Eggelston, Forrest W. Galey, Evan Gargiulo, Hadley Gilman, Tom Gitterman, Howard Greenberg, J. Richard Gruber, Ann Hawthorne, Leigh Hendry, Steve Henry, Susan Henry, Edwynn Houk, Jenni Holder, Lisa Kurts, Scott Ledbetter, David Lusk, Karen Marks, Deborah Miller, Laurence Miller, Millie Moorhead, Katie Neyman, Donald Polk, Dan Pomeroy, Yancey Richardson, Pam Roberts, Grace Rothstein, Melissa Taylor, David Thompson, Takouhy Wise, Warren Woods, and Helen Wright.

I am greatly indebted to the writers in the catalogue - Peter Guralnick, Deborah Willis Kennedy, Charles Reagan Wilson, Bill Wyman, and John Grisham - for their insightful contributions that bring so much to the understanding and interpretation of the images herein as well as to the culture of the American South and the blues. I am especially grateful to Richard Havers for bringing Bill Wyman's interest in the South to my attention and for his valuable knowledge and experience of blues culture. Merry and Frank Thomasson, who brought their publishing experience to the project, and Renee and John Grisham are to be commended for their efforts in bringing the catalogue to reality. Calvin Foster brought his fresh aesthetics, intuition, and design expertise resulting in a visually intriguing, user-friendly book; he was assisted in its production by Hugh Busby and Karla Merritt. Charles Miers and Jessica Fuller gave significant advice throughout the book's production. Many thanks go to Paul Bray, Joan DePaoli, and Anne Ellegood for their editorial advice and assistance and their encouragement at critical moments.

Finally, I am most grateful for the support and forbearance shown to me by my family - James, Glynnis, and Blaise - during the development and production of *Visualizing the Blues*. Their good cheer, faith, and encouragement were essential to the project's completion. There are countless others whose contribution to this project are also deeply appreciated.

clarence john laughlin (1905-1985), *Elegy for the Old South, #2*, 1941

ralston crawford (1906 - 1978), *Iron Fence, New Orleans, 1959*

james j. kamm

Music takes us out of the actual and whispers to us dim secrets that startle our wonder as to who we are, and for what, whence, and whereto.
    –Ralph Waldo Emerson

Visualizing the Blues spans almost the entire history of photography in America and documents the life of the Mississippi Delta and its people.

The stories that these images tell us run the gamut of human experience. Some tell us compelling tales of life at its hardest, while others celebrate the love of the land and the shared joys of human interaction. Together, the photographs in this exhibition paint a portrait of the Delta, giving expression both to the land's lushness and to the generative nature of its people.

George Gershwin, one of America's most original and influential composers, said, "True music must repeat the thought and inspirations of the people. My people are Americans and my time is today." The same can be said for the Mississippi Delta and its vital contributions to American music. The culture of the South that gave birth to the blues also inspired the photographers in this exhibition to come to the Delta and capture its character on film.

The Mississippi Delta has been called the "Fertile Crescent of American Music" because it was here that the blues were born. Emerging from the field hollers of slave laborers with rich African musical traditions, the blues grew into a music that is distinctively American.

In the decades after the Civil War and in several waves of migration during the first half of the 20th century, Southerners left their homes in the Delta in search of a better life. Carrying the music of the Delta with them, the children of the South swelled the populations of cities like St. Louis, Chicago, and Detroit, and they changed the culture of those cities, and the country itself, forever.

But why stop there? Globalization has given us, for better or for worse, a world culture where American contributions reign supreme. The blues and its children – gospel, jazz, rock 'n' roll – are known and appreciated the world over. Today, it is not hard to find major blues festivals taking place in all corners of the globe – Europe, South America, Japan, Australia – at any time of the year.

Musicologist and critic George Jellinek said, "The history of a people is found in its songs." The blues played so critical a role in the development of American, and indeed the world's, music that the history of the Mississippi Delta and the history of the United States are inextricably linked. The creativity and inventiveness of the people of the Delta are appreciated the world over.

Visualizing the Blues is an important exhibition for The Dixon Gallery and Gardens. As the preeminent visual arts institution in Memphis, Tennessee, the "Capital of the Delta," the Dixon is the heart of the expansive and culturally vibrant Mid-South region. The exhibition, the catalogue, and the wide array of interpretive programs surrounding the show are the product of a collaboration that spans the Mid-South and underscores the unity of spirit that binds together the people of the Delta. We are grateful to The University of Mississippi's Center for the Study of Southern Culture; The University of Memphis; The Blues Foundation; The Center for Southern Folklore; The Memphis Charitable Foundation; The Greater Memphis Arts Council; The National Civil Rights Museum; The Memphis Black Repertory Theater; The Oakwood Arts & Sciences Charitable Trust; and the Memphis Convention & Visitors Bureau for their generous assistance with this extraordinary project.

I would particularly like to thank the many people who made *Visualizing the Blues* possible. First and foremost, I am grateful to the show's curator, Wendy McDaris, for it was her passionate belief in and commitment to the project, and her discerning eye that was responsible for the layered richness of the exhibition and the quality of this publication. Working closely with Wendy on the exhibition were Anne Ellegood and the Dixon's assistant curator Vivian Kung-Haga, registrar Neil O'Brien, executive assistant, Sally Kee, and Deborah Bass Gibbs. Without them, this project would not have been possible. I admire their dedication and sense of professionalism and I am deeply appreciative of their hard work.

One of the things that makes *Visualizing the Blues* so special is the rich array of programs that the Dixon's education coordinator, Jane Faquin, developed to enhance and interpret the exhibition. Multi-dimensional and multi-talented, Jane played a critical role in the design and implementation of every program and event surrounding the presentation of *Visualizing the Blues* at the Dixon – the *Visualizing the Blues Symposium 2000;* the exhibition's video programs; and the concert and film series. Jane also worked closely with the Greater Memphis Arts Council and The Blues Foundation on the development of educational programs and curricula, which complemented the "Blues in the Schools Programs" for elementary and middle schools throughout the Mid-South. Jane's assistance with the Memphis Black Repertory Theater's production of *Robert Johnson: Trick the Devil* helped to make this wonderful collaboration a memorable experience for all involved.

The installation of *Visualizing the Blues* at the Dixon bore the mark of three very talented and sensitive individuals, two of whom, James Starks and Robert Jones, are on the Dixon's staff, and the third, David White, an artist in Memphis, who routinely helps with installations and a variety of other projects. These three men worked closely with Wendy McDaris and our curatorial staff. Together, they achieved a wonderfully balanced and sophisticated presentation of the material in the exhibition, and I praise their many skills.

I want to thank director of development, Russell Ingram, for his tireless efforts to secure funding for the exhibition and its attendant programs, and for directing the marketing and special membership programs, which helped make *Visualizing the Blues* accessible to so many throughout the Mid-South.

While I mentioned here only a handful of the Dixon's staff, the *Visualizing the Blues* project, in all its parts, was the result of the shared commitment and hard work of every member of the staff, and I am grateful to them all.

In addition to the Dixon's staff, I would like to thank a number of individuals from other organizations and institutions who played a critical role in making *Visualizing the Blues* a success. Charles Reagan Wilson, Director of the University of Mississippi's Center for the Study of Southern Culture and Howard Stovall, Director, and Pat Mitchell of the Blues Foundation deserve special recognition, as do Judy Peiser, Director, Deni Carr and Tommy McReynolds of the Center for Southern Folklore; Beverly Robertson, Director of the National Civil Rights Museum; David Evans, Professor of Music at the University of Memphis; Kenneth Goings, Historian at the University of Memphis; John Lawrence, Director of Museum Programs at The Historic New Orleans Collection; Jeffrey Nesin,

President of Memphis College of Art; Rick Gruber, Director of The Ogden Museum of Southern Art; Trey Giutine, Guest Services Manager at Mississippi River Museum at Mud Island Park; Pat Kerr Tigrett, President of the Memphis Charitable Foundation; Kevin Kane, Director, and the staff of the Memphis Convention and Visitors Bureau; and finally, Bill Ferris, Chairman of the National Endowment for the Humanities. I am grateful to these individuals for their keen intrest in the blues and for their valuable advice and counsel. *Visualizing the Blues* was a far richer experience for their generous collaboration.

Others, who gave much appreciated advice are William Shepherd, Jim Czarniecki, David Porter, Lawson Apperson, and John and Renee Grisham.

The essays in this book paint a wonderfully creative picture of the Delta and its people, and of the impact and importance of its music. I wish to thank Wendy McDaris, Peter Guralnick, Deborah Willis Kennedy, Charles Reagan Wilson and John Grisham for their enormous contributions to this publication. For their expertise and talent in producing this publication, I am grateful to Frank and Merry Thomasson, and to Calvin Foster for the book's distinctive design, and to photographer, Pete Ceren.

William Bearden's writing and production of the exhibition's video programs deserve our heartfelt thanks and appreciation; and many thanks also to Eddie Dattel of Inside Sounds for his production of the *Visualizing the Blues* CD.

Of course, the exhibition would not have been possible were it not for the generosity of the institutions and individuals who lent works to the show, and I extend my special thanks to the photographers who loaned their works and provided valuable advice and insights throughout the process of planning this exhibition and publication. A complete listing of all of the lenders to the exhibition is to be found elsewhere in this publication.

Finally, I would like to thank the generous corporations and foundations that sponsored *Visualizing the Blues,* the catalogue, and the extraordinary complement of interpretive programs. We are grateful to First Tennessee's Bravo Series for its generous support, and we are very proud to have been the recipient of one of the largest grants ever awarded by this prestigious philanthropic program. We are also thankful for the generous support of Smith & Nephew; LEDIC Management Group; Buckeye Technologies; Ernst & Young LLP; The Hyde Family Foundations; Northwest Airlines; The American Express Company; Horseshoe Casino; The Oakwood Arts & Sciences Charitable Trust; and the Memphis Charitable Foundation.

Additional assistance and support for this project came from the Memphis Flyer, Time Warner and News Radio WREC, our media sponsors; and for framing and reproduction services, we are grateful to The Art Dept., Inc.; Larson Juhl Custom Frames; and The Chrome Lab, inc. We thank you all.

James J. Kamm
Director,
The Dixon Gallery and Gardens

sally mann (b. 1951), *Untitled 1998 from the Deep South series*, 1998

john grisham

Why has so much music come from the South? And so many writers? What is it in the water down there that inspires so much?

These questions have been kicked about for decades, but the answer is really quite easy. Simply put, the South has better material.

The South began and expanded slavery, fought and lost a war, suffered through Reconstruction, languished through decades of poverty, and resisted change at every pivotal moment in history. Its wounds were self-inflicted, but so very colorful. Suffering gave rise to creativity.

A hundred years ago, in the heart of the Mississippi Delta, an impoverished region so hard and cruel that most who got the chance fled and seldom looked back, the blues were born. Raw, simple, emotional, the blues expressed the harshness of life in that tortured locale. Its first artists sang and played not for money or appeal, but simply for themselves. Their music soothed them; it was their escape.

Obviously, the blues were and are meant to be heard. So the notion of visualizing them may at first seem a bit odd. But look at the photographs that follow, and you will see from whom and from where the blues came. You will see the places - the juke joints and cotton fields and country stores and ramshackle houses and rural churches. You will even see the poverty and severity of life that made folks turn to song to forget their troubles. You will see the hatred and violence that plagued the region, though the music has seldom dwelt on these subjects. You will see the drinking and dancing and dice - the small pleasures of a hard life. And you will see the faces of those who inspired the others to sing.

The blues can never be captured by photography, or motion picture, or written word. But through this remarkable collection, you can see and almost feel the sweltering history of the birth-place of the blues.

huger foote (b. 1961), *Cooper and Southern, 1995*

william eggleston (b. 1939), *Untitled, c. 1965*

wendy mcdaris

The blues is an apt analogy for the American South's complex culture. Every shade of human emotion can be found in the blues, many lyrics of which are powerful poems bearing a singular and refined economy of expression. The music itself is sophisticated and engaging. Robert Johnson, considered a titan among bluesmen, left a legacy as the most influential among the musicians of the genre. The story of his life is the stuff of myth and parallels the pervasive mystery that haunts the streets of a host of southern towns and permeates Southern landscapes. Many bluesmen have become legends globally – Charley Patton, Robert Jr. Lockwood, Skip James, Johnny Shines, Muddy Waters, Howlin' Wolf, Sonny Boy Williamson, Son House, John Lee Hooker, and Jimmy Reed. The obstacles they overcame to carry their messages to the rest of the world qualify them as heroic figures. That they dared to bring their music to the public and eventually to the world stage made them forerunners of a new age in the American South.

Like bluesmen, Southern writers are recognized globally. So much has been said and written about their literary contributions that simply mentioning the genre is enough to call up impressions of its innovative styles, haunting narratives, and eccentric characters. Interestingly, author Edgar Allan Poe, often considered a Northern writer and one of America's great literary figures, shares an ambiance and subject matter with Southern writers in his own work and for good reason. Poe spent his formative years, up to the age of nineteen, in Virginia as the stepson of John Allan. They had a difficult relationship particularly after the death of Poe's mother. Eventually he was disowned by his stepfather and completely estranged from his Southern heritage. Literary critic Paul Bray believes Poe's upbringing during the era of slavery in Virginia was in large part responsible for the immersion of Poe's psyche in melancholia and despair and his obsession with mortality. Bray maintains Poe's reflection of those concerns in his poetry and prose qualifies him as the South's greatest antebellum writer. Contemporary southern writers - Toni Morrison, Alice Walker, Larry Brown, Dorothy Allison and Randall Kenan among many - pay homage to the spiritual ambiance, graces and somberness of Poe's South while focusing on matters heretofore only alluded to, such as traditions and customs of African-American society, tentative if not open exchanges between races, a tenacious poverty that breeds violence out of desperation, spirituality, faith, and a belief in the occult that appear to be woven into the fabric of everyday life.

Part of the South's appeal is attributable to the historically dominant African and Celtic cultures whose similarities include longstanding religious and spiritual traditions augmented by a variety of imaginative superstitions, strong musical and dance heritages, a history of oral storytelling, tribal roots, and, interestingly, a shared oppression by the English. A third group of people, often overlooked but an important part of the South's early history, were significant contributors to the culture of the blues. Arriving from England, many of them from its northern regions, these people were oppressed by the English as well, having previously been imprisoned, sold into indentured slavery, or simply deemed "unwanted" and given no alternative but to sail for America. This early cultural mix produced over time an undeniably new culture that was thrust early on in its history, for over a century, into momentous debates, devastating war, and far-reaching social struggles.

For these reasons among others, the South has frequently been perceived as a society of extremes and such a perception has left it vulnerable to oversimplification. Hollywood has mined this vulnerability successfully. The most recognized production in this vein is *Gone with the Wind* which still thrills movie audiences sixty years after its initial showing with depictions of an idiosyncratic, demanding aristocracy with unique codes of decorum, a cult of warriors, a penchant for the emotional and high-spirited, and a slave class with a propensity for artifice and superstition. Later in the 1960s, Paul Newman played a Hollywood archetype, the southern pretty-boy, career criminal, and prison system hard-case, in *Cool Hand Luke*. James Dickey's novel *Deliverance* depicted an unknowable, unpredictable, unsavory South where backwoods hillbillies preyed on unwitting outdoorsmen. There are many more examples but the reality is, of course, that southern culture is complex and highly nuanced.

Mystery Train, Jim Jarmusch's 1990 mythic portrait of Memphis, offers a contemporary read on southern culture as enigmatic, an indecipherable cipher. In the film, a string of delays, miscalculations, and serious misadventures detain an Italian widow, young Japanese tourists, and a despondent laborer from the United Kingdom and his Southern cohorts in the maze that is Memphis' underbelly. All of them secure overnight accommodations at a downtown fleabag hotel where a night manager, played very remarkably by Screamin' Jay Hawkins, and a bell boy create distractions of the most insignificant kind in an effort to fend off extreme boredom. Elvis' ghost presides over all. The lights of a downtown as unattainable as Oz glitter in the distance. Only the train moving through the city conveys a sense of purpose. This is a place that time and commerce have forgotten, a place of dreams and fairy tales, scams and crimes, low-key pleasures and intolerable frustrations, abandoned buildings and weeds growing up through sidewalks, an urban sphinx amid a desert of perplexing and eloquent visions. From this strange environment emerge prescient mythologies announced not by the blaring of trumpets but by the strumming of guitars. *Mystery Train* is as significant a symbol of the new South as *Gone With The Wind* is exemplary of how many Americans viewed the old South. Jarmusch's vision redefines Southern culture as a cultivator of dreamers, thinkers, a site where a small scale miracle may grow to thunderous consequence, an inexplicable site possessing many shades of gray between its black and white extremes.

From its inception a medium with a parallel spectrum of grays, photography has had a convoluted relationship with the South. Both medium and culture have developed together over a span of 160 years and, beginning with the year 1852, the exhibit collection for *Visualizing the Blues* reveals intervals during which the two parallel histories converge to mutually illuminating effect. Some of the images exemplify technological advances and formal and conceptual issues that have engaged artists throughout the history of photography while simultaneously recognizing that the South, as a subject and a site, has played a profoundly significant and inspirational role in that history. As photography grappled with its own developmental issues, America observed a distilled, more urgent version of its own troubling issues reflected in the socio-economic and political turbulence weathered by the South beginning with The Civil War. Thus, this collection comprises a visual record of a culture with a controversial and difficult past, the strength and determination to endure that past and re-imagine itself, and the ability to contribute a particularly weighty measure to the national character.

Historians have long debated a division between the "old" South and the "new"

South, placing it variously at the time of The Civil War and points beyond but often around the turn of the 19th century. Taken together, the photographs in *Visualizing the Blues* allude to a transition, a growing away from the old and into the new that is marked first by degrees of intensity and turmoil and a sense that there was much that ought to be changed, and subsequently by degrees of coolness that draw inspiration from more subjective and formally engaged perspectives.

Viewed chronologically, a series of images about the Ku Klux Klan by W. Eugene Smith, William Christenberry, and Andres Serrano exemplifies this shift from old to new, from passionately hot to analytically cool. W. Eugene Smith's shot c. 1951-58, *KKK Grandmother*, shows an elderly woman in satin KKK garb standing against a night sky. Behind her a man, also in a KKK costume, appears to be wearing a pair of glasses with a plastic nose and fake mustache attached. The image plays emotional ping pong with the viewer as the figures, being both sinister and surreal, contradict themselves. One figure is unexpectedly an elderly woman whose participation challenges typical grandmotherly traits. The symbolic meaning of the cross on her costume twists in upon itself. The other figure is frightening and laughable, both a representation of inconceivable violence and disdain and, at the same time, a character not to be taken seriously.

In 1982, William Christenberry constructed the image of a Klansman by clothing a G.I. Joe doll in a KKK costume. The impact of the photograph, one from the series *From The Klan Room, 1982*, relies on half-obscured details - a tiny, plastic hand peeks out impotently from a white sleeve and neon eyes glow from the pointed hood like an alien. The knowledge that the costume conceals a G.I. Joe doll carries national as well as regional implications, an important notion since the KKK, frequently considered an organization operating in the Southern states, concentrates its efforts today in areas well outside the South.

As with W. Eugene Smith's work, Andres Serrano's selection of a woman for his 1990 portrait, *Klanswoman (Grand Klaliff II),* is initially more shocking than if the subject were male. The similarity ends there, however. In Serrano's work the woman's hood is only partially seen, resulting in a deliberate diminishment of it's symbolic power since the hood carries less import without its point. Instead, the composition and color of the image overshadow the potential impact of the now infamous KKK attire, transmogrifying the expression in her one exposed eye from that of conviction to that of uncertainty. Serrano's *Klanswoman* is a powerful formal work that essentially robs the subject of its ability to incite the fear and dread with which the Ku Klux Klan has customarily been associated. The use of this striking formal strategy underscores the power of art in a poignant contrast to that of political hate groups.

Similarly, Eudora Welty's set of portraits that pairs an African-American farmer sitting on his front porch near two watermelons he has grown with a white dry goods store owner seated next to watermelons in his storefront window, elicits responses that center around differences in the subjects' lives as well as questions of race. The farmer's more natural pose outside his home discloses a life sustained by living simply and close to the land. The portrait of the storekeeper, a proprietary hand resting on one of the watermelons beside him, reveals a regimented life through his posture and expression. The pain and dignity in both faces are equally affecting, for they have a common source - skin color. The watermelons become an essential descriptive element in each portrait and, in terms of how they are treated in their respective photographs, eloquent symbols of economic class drawn on color lines.

Ashley T. Mitchell's photograph *Untitled (Woman with Vegetables, Olive Branch, Mississippi)*, 1998, is an interesting contrast to the Welty portraits. Mitchell's subject, a woman walking across her yard with an armful of freshly picked vegetables, comprises an ode to the sweltering summer heat at midday, its role in the potential of the earth in that region, and the small tasks that fill a life lived close to the land. The function of the woman in the photograph has less to do with who she is than what she has been doing only seconds ago. The yard is a glimpsed explanation rather than a studied commentary. The "in-between" expression on the woman's face obviates *the moment* in opposition to *the momentous*.

Historical photographs, whether of the momentous or ordinary, often appear masterful in a contemporary context. Historical photographs of the South are exceptionally good references for understanding this phenomenon. For instance, *Richmond, Virginia, Ruins of the Gallego Flour Mills,* April 1865, by Alexander Gardner is a record of the systematic and thorough destruction from which the South took decades to recover. At the time it was taken, this piece of photographic journalism must have had a devastating effect on Southerners. A contemporary audience without knowledge of the narrative behind the image, however, may well find the work compositionally compelling, surreal even. Viewing ancient ruins in Piranesi's Baroque era engravings, Hubert Robert's Rococo paintings, or numerous Romantic paintings of the 19th century elicits a similar response. Thus, the image speaks to its present audience through form and mood rather than through the passionate content of its own time.

Another phenomenon associated with time's relationship to photography can be demonstrated by images of portentous events that document social injustice. In such instances, a photograph may serve not only as witness, but also as a harbinger of change thereby accelerating the process of social justice. It is impossible to accurately gauge the influence of such photographs in their own time, but there is no denying the impact even today of pictures such as Danny Lyon's *The Movement, 1964* that shows a clash between a demonstrator and a policeman as onlookers stand by in the background. The commitment to the Civil Rights Movement and the boiling desperation on either side of the issue is herein made palpable. With its far-reaching implications for the nation's future, *The Movement* functioned as evidence of the passionate struggle taking place at that time and predicted the inevitability of change. In a contemporary context, the image marks a transitional milestone that, viewed together with other photographs of a socially urgent nature, describes the South's transit from the darkness of slave-holding times to wars and battles over the legacy of slavery. This is the South that would ultimately emerge as a culture constructed on the basis of assessments and admissions of the past and which would thus have great potential for an enlightened future.

There are also themes in which images taken over a succession of decades show vacillation. This state is perhaps the truest reflection of how a culture metamorphoses over time, incremental step by incremental step, sometimes moving ahead, at times reverting to previous positions. Images of inmates in the Southern prison system are exemplary. Southern prisons have been especially difficult destinations in which to serve out a sentence. It is not surprising that prison is a popular subject in photography as it is in the lyrics of the blues. Margaret Bourke-White's work entitled *Hood's Chapel, Georgia, 1936*, shows a prisoner resting from field work wearing a typical striped suit. Tellingly, he carries a spoon behind one of the iron bands that encircles his legs while his hands are clasped gracefully across his chest. Though his face is in a state of utter repose, the tensed leg pressing against a rock reveals a constant awareness of his circumstances. The varied oblique lines pulling against one another – the striped prison suits and the light jaggedly dividing the image's surface – reinforce this awareness.

It is a great wonder that inmates could find any sort of pleasure in a prison environment, but somehow they do in Jack Delano's *Convicts in the County Jail, Green County, Georgia, June 1941*. A dancer in typical striped attire struts effeminately to guitar music as other prisoners keep time by clapping their hands. There is irony in this image as, astonishingly, prisoners find sufficient joy left within themselves to dance and play music in this stark and cruel environment.

Just the *names* of certain prisons can inspire fear and dread, i.e., Angola in Louisiana or Parchman in Mississippi. Their reputations for cruelty and tough prisoners are well known even among the general public. Deborah Luster marks a departure from the prison images previously discussed by evoking the age-old institution of human warehousing through the use of tin type technology in *One Big Self: Prisoners of Louisiana,* 1999. Despite the severe constraints placed on their lives, one senses hope, pride and solidarity among Luster's composite of Louisiana's current inmate population.

A similar irony imbues photographs taken by Walker Evans and Peter Sekaer during the Farm Security Administration era from 1930-38. The FSA directed photographers to focus on the difficult living conditions in rural America. The South, with its already weakened post-Civil War economy compounded by the stock market crash of 1929, was a particularly convincing site in this regard. Evans' ground breaking image *Kitchen Wall, Alabama Farmstead, 1936,* reveals the objectivity which became a hallmark of his style. In this image Evans selected elements that came together formally rather than choosing to underscore the poignancy of lives lived with so little, though there were times when he did so. Additionally, this interior demonstrates photography's unique ability for achieving visual democracy; it can blur the division between what is considered beautiful or plain, worthy of attention or unremarkable.

Like Evans, Peter Sekaer, a Danish immigrant, traveled to the South between 1930 and 1938. His *Untitled (Cow and Chicken Painted on Wall),* c. 1935, an image of animal heads painted on the outside brick wall of a butcher shop, transforms primitive line drawings into a series of elements in a powerfully framed abstract composition. It evidences Sekaer's engagement with formal considerations and the inherent distance such an engagement implies. Both Sekaer and Evans were also inspired by the simplicity and directness of Southern life perhaps because it is in the South that the business of living rather than high commerce has historically been and still is overtly in evidence. They also seemed to appreciate the unselfconscious tradition of making things by hand that continues to lend a certain quaintness and individuality to the face of the South.

Contemporary photographer James Perry Walker steps back a few paces in *Gathering Eggs, 1979* to enjoy the intersection of the formal and the handmade in much the same way Evans and Sekaer did. The image's narrative, gathering eggs, is subsumed by the synergy of horizontals, obliques, and verticals that contrast with the static figure on the ladder and the hen scurrying madly out of the way. In all three of the aforementioned images one finds an austere beauty, a result of the photographers' emotional distance from their subjects. Evans' farmstead wall and Sekaer's brick butcher shop wall foreshadow a shift in focus from narrative to form for photographers of the South beginning with the advent of color photography as a fine art practice at mid-century.

It seems appropriate that color fine art photography was legitimized in part by two southern pioneers in the field, William Christenberry and William Eggleston. Like black-and-white photographers before them, Christenberry and Eggleston utilized the South as an especially rich source for imagery. Though it is evident their oeuvres take much inspiration from the cool distance apparent in much of Walker Evans' work, there is an important difference between these two and many of those before them who photographed the South. Photography critic Gerry Badger coined the term "quiet" to describe this difference. In such images the subject, almost always a modest one, is shot without technical tricks or contrived and elaborate sets, and presented in a self-effacing way. This is probably the most accommodating and appropriate way to capture the South because as a culture, it, too, frequently presents itself honestly, straightforwardly, and, on occasion, humorously. While Christenberry's work has deviated from this "quiet" style through the use of sets, dramatic lighting, and loaded imagery, Eggleston has built his career on it.

Indeed, Eggleston's work generated a good deal of controversy when it was first shown by The Museum of Modern Art, New York, in 1976, and was criticized for being inconsequential. At the same time, the South was under-valued except, as usual, in the area of popular music. *Untitled, 1980* is a brilliant example of Eggleston's dressed down, sophisticated, highly influential vision. It comprises an homage to the simple kitchen interior often encountered in Southern residences. A hushed unpretentiousness pervades the scene right down to the "essentials" stacked neatly at one end of the expansive table top - a mostly smoked pack of cigarettes, an inexpensive brand of hot sauce, salt and pepper housed in bottles that may have contained other spices at one time. To the left are three partially filled shelves with under utilized divided spaces at the top. The sky blue wall ends its paint haphazardly as if the painter were called away for something more pleasurable like fishing, hunting, or just plain sitting on the porch. Light glances off the corner of a metal chair back prompting memories of late afternoon sunlight and contented solitude. Eggleston pairs the plain with the elegantly spare. In so doing, he conjures the essence of the culture. Photography of such eloquence, depth, and reflective power cannot fail to generate its own following.

Portraits of Southerners frequently show them in a reflective or contemplative mode. Contemporary photographer Nicholas Nixon's *Yazoo City, Mississippi, 1979*, introduces the viewer to an African-American father and his young daughter. The downward gaze of the father deflects the attention of the camera while the daughter directs her gaze pointedly towards the lens. There is an unexpected bestowal of strength and confidence in the child in peculiar contrast to the father's diffidence which belies his adulthood and sinewy, mature physique. Part of this photograph's genius lies in its modest presentation as it simultaneously sets up a discourse on social, generational, gender and political issues.

Elizabeth Says Goodbye, Greenville, Mississippi, 1993 is Jane Rule Burdine's ode to a woman's remembrance of her life spent in rural Mississippi. The sitter is a study in tranquility as she gazes out over a garden in glorious bloom to a point well beyond earthly concerns; two months later she would pass away. Like the raised portraits on Roman coins, her genteel profile leaves an impression of strength, courage, and endurance. Mark Steinmetz uncovers a similar distance in a teenage girl's expression in *Athens, Georgia, 1996.* Lying on the hood of a car with her head resting against the windshield, she stares dreamily down a small town street on a summer evening. Hope, uncertainty, and ennui linger in her look while youthful charm and prettiness are emphasized by her apparent inattention to these attributes and her nonchalant demeanor.

Indeed, the degree to which portraits appear to be posed or spontaneous raise ethical questions such as photography's utility as propaganda. Many portraits made for the FSA were purportedly the product of multiple takes and manipulations of sitters and settings in a zealous effort to capture rural poverty; some of these portraits are considered icons of the photographic medium and greatly symbolic of their time. During the same era, however, Doris Ulmann made a photograph of a gathering of four men during a religious foot washing ritual. Their rapt expressions are a visual definition of grace. Large dapples of light fall on a shoulder, the side of a face, the top of a head. The viewer is drawn into the intimate circle of participants by Ulmann's signature combination of empathy and respect that cancels out her presence as mediator. Ulmann's "absence" is one of the qualities indicative of mastery of the medium.

Despite contemporary practices that result in "photo hybrids" such as computer enhancements that transform photographs into versions of other media, the documentary nature of photography continues to be both the camera's backbone and drawback as an artistic tool. As understanding and appreciation for photography has flourished particularly since the 1970s, so, too, has an appreciation of the South's deep, vibrant culture. A host of photographers, young and not so young, have emerged with new images of the South and the long-standing relationship between the culture and the medium has deepened. Interestingly, these new images are unabashedly documentary in style while at the same time mesmerizing the viewer with a multitude of conceptual and formal aspects. For example, Allison Nowlin immortalizes an important Southern symbol in her image of a well-used, dearly loved pickup truck parked at night under New Orleans street lamps. David Julian Leonard shoots a half-eaten bar-b-que sandwich and can of soda lit by sun rays that pierce through an abstract open brick pattern, giving this most popular of Southern foods a religious aura. William Greiner's image of a television floating in a bayou is both astoundingly sophisticated in formal terms with its spectrum of beiges and play of light and oblique lines, and referentially witty as Louisiana's answer to Elvis Presley's legendary television screen shooting. Tseng Kwong Chi stands with military stiffness in a Mao suit and mirrored aviator glasses before the gates of Graceland, one of a number of "wonders of the world" in front of which the artist has felt compelled to make self- portraits. Patty Carroll shoots a humble Sun Studio amid the silence that befalls downtown Memphis at night under the solar brightness of a corner street lamp. Huger Foote walks the viewer through a thick curtain of sensual, dripping wisteria amongst which reds, golds and greens vibrate and create a metaphorical positive. Maude Schuyler Clay's landscape, *To The Memory of Emmett Till, Cassidy Bayou, Sumner, Tallahatchie County, Mississippi, 1998,* absorbs the darkest moments of the past in the mournful grace of a woods that hugs the bank of a creek in the quickening evening and gently coaxes from its shadows the promise of a new morning.

For the South, the seeds of that morning were sown far back in the past in its haunted landscape that later sustained an agrarian economy. Thus, the region has managed to maintain its disposition towards the business of living rather than the business of business, and refutes the market place as the most important factor in the determination of happiness. Its fondness for, nay, indulgence towards what is individual and eccentric safeguard it from slickness and homogeneity. To this day, on Southern city streets or country roads one may still observe lone pedestrians whistling or singing as they walk in a manner that resembles a dance step more than a gait, not because they are mad but out of the sheer joy of being alive. Perhaps this is due in part from *collective* knowledge of hard times and how to survive them. It is a place where life is still slow enough to allow the mind to assume a naturally receptive state and where contemplatives are not only tolerated but nurtured and celebrated. Its unrelenting reality has required of the South an unshakable spirituality capable of wresting *what is* out of *what could be*.

Photographers have reveled in Southern visions because photography shares certain fundamental characteristics with the culture. There is something Duchampian about the "ready-made" physical environment of the South and its role in "straight" photography's approach to image-making. Photography is mysterious in its process. It's explicit power originates from concepts such as *truth* and *reality*, while ambivalence, subtlety, and numerous shades of meaning are its support structure. Not only does it obfuscate the differences between document and implication, reality and memory, art and artifact, truth and the imagined, it weaves them together in a whole fabric. Ambiguity endows photography with the power to elicit a hypnotic state. As a result photography, like the blues, is subversive and transcendental at the same time.

clarence john laughlin (1905-1985), *Magnificent Avenue, Number One*, 1947

william christenberry (b.1936), *Abandoned House in Field, Near Montgomery, Alabama, 1971, 1971*

anonymous , *Catherine Hunt, Black Slave Woman, Holding her Mistress' Baby, Julia Hunt*, 1852

marion post wolcott   (1910-1990), *Resting from Hoeing Cotton,on the Allen Plantation, a F.S.A. Cooperative, Natchitoches, Louisiana,* 1940

eudora welty (b.1909), *Grenada County,* c. 1930's

eudora welty (b.1909), *Storekeeper, Rankin County, Mississippi,* c. 1935

clarence john laughlin (1905-1985), *Elegy for Moss Land,* 1940

alain desvergnes (b.1931), *(series on)* *"YOKNAPATAWPHA" 1963-1965 The World of Faulkner, 1963*

margaret bourke-white (1904-1971), *Hood's Chapel, Georgia,1936*

alexander gardner (1821-1882), *Antietam, Maryland, Confederate Dead by a Fence on Hagerstown Road, September 1862*

anonymous, *With Most of Their Men Folk Away at the Front, Women Ran the Plantations During the Civil War, These Are All Slaves, 1863,* 1863

gordon parks (b.1912), *William Causey's Son with Gun During Violence in Alabama*, 1956

maude schuyler clay (b.1953), *To the Memory of Emmett Till, Cassidy Bayou, Sumner, Tallahatchie County, Mississippi, 1998,* 1998

jack spencer (b.1951), *Sheldon Church Ruins (burned by General Sherman 1865), Sheldon, South Carolina, 1998*, 1998

dorothea lange (1895-1965), *Lunchtime for Cotton Hoers, Mississippi Delta*, June 1937

tom rankin (b.1957), *St. James M. B. Church, Jonestown, 1991*

larry e. mcpherson (b.1943), *Mississippi River from Chickasaw Bluff #2, Tipton County, TN, 1998*

dorothea lange (1895-1965), *Cotton Picker, Eutaw, Alabama, c. 1939*

david julian leonard (b.1962), *Elephant's Graveyard*, 1996

jane rule burdine (b.1946), *Willow Run Hunting Club, Hollandale, Mississippi, 1988*

william christenberry (b. 1936), *Window of Palmist Building, Havana Junction, Alabama, 1981, 1981*

peter guralnick

What have we got, then, when all is said and done? A few "facts," indistinguishable, really, from the "facts" of many bluesmen's lives. Some anecdotes, embellished perhaps over the years. A portrait of a young man who "didn't talk too much," was "moody," was perceived by whites as unsure of himself and by his peers as a rambler, a showman, but a "lone wolf" who, in Johnny Shines's words, was "close only to his own guitar." He was "friendly," he was "neat," he spoke little about his family or his past (but then, one wonders, who did?), he was well liked but little-known. Perhaps the best summation comes in Johnny Shines's description of his friend as "very bashful but very imposing." Polite, self-effacing, unreadable—destined to remain as much of a mystery, as much of a phantom, in Mack McCormick's conceit, as he was before a single fact was known or a single document unearthed. The sources of his art will likewise remain a mystery.

The parallels to Shakespeare are in many ways striking. The towering achievement. The shadowy presence. The critical dissent that great art cannot come from a person so uneducated. The way in which each could cannibalize tradition and create a synthesis that is certainly recognizable in its sources and yet somehow altogether and wholly original. I am not arguing that Robert Johnson's art has a Shakespearean scope; nor is he a lost figure in an epic tradition, as some romanticists would suggest. As a lyric poet, though, he occupies a unique position where he can very much stand on his own.

His music remains equally unique. Not that it cannot be placed within a definable tradition, vigorously carried on by Muddy Waters and Johnny Shines, among others. But there was something about his music that seemed to strike all who listened, so that even a professional musician like Henry Townsend—on friendly terms with recording stars like

Roosevelt Sykes and Lonnie Johnson—would express his awe at Robert's technique and execution. Most accounts agree he rarely practiced. "When he picked up his guitar, he picked it up for business," says Johnny Shines. According to both Shines and Robert Lockwood he was extremely reluctant to expose new material in public. Women with whom he stayed described to Mack McCormick how they would wake up in the middle of the night to discover him fingering the guitar strings almost soundlessly at the window by the light of the moon. If he realized that they were awake, he would stop almost immediately, a detail which corresponds with the many accounts of how he would shield his hands or turn away if he felt that another musician's eyes were on him while he was playing. He liked to play solo for the most part, though Townsend describes working out parts with him and Johnny Shines says that on certain songs he welcomed a complement and had decided ideas of what part he wanted the second guitar to play. Most observers agree that he generally played his songs the same way each time; it might be that before he had a song worked out he would experiment with different voicings, but for the most part, once the song was set, neither accompaniment nor vocal effects varied a great deal. His was a very clearly thought-out approach, then, but where he got his initial conception from no one seems to know. "He was a great guy for plain inspiration," Henry Townsend told Pete Welding. "He'd get a feeling, and out of nowhere he could put a song together.... I remember asking him about songs he had sung two or three nights before, and he'd tell me, well, he wouldn't, he couldn't do that one again. And I'd ask him why. He'd say, 'Well, that was just a feeling. I was just, just . . . reciting from a feeling.'"

What made his music so different from that of his contemporaries is equally a mystery. You can point to Hambone Willie Newbern, whose "Rollin' and Tumblin'" melody (actually a traditional piece, which was first recorded by Newbern) was the inspiration for many of Johnson's songs; you can point to Son House, Johnson's closest influence, or Charley Patton, an equally emotive performer. The music of more apparently sophisticated guitarists like Scrapper Blackwell and, of course, Lonnie Johnson, shows up again and again in his work, and his style of slide guitar playing was a commonplace in the Delta. And yet there was something altogether unique and immediately recognizable about the way in which Robert Johnson transmuted all these familiar elements, adapted them to the nervous, edgy style that critic Whitney Balliett once called "rough" and "wild-animal"-like. Perhaps this was the very source of his attraction: the seeming tension between a fiery emotionalism barely on the edge of control and a masterful sense of technique. Johnny Shines has been most eloquent in describing the effect of his music as well as its accomplishments.

According to Shines: "Robert came along with the walking bass, the boogie bass, and using diminished chords that were not built in one form. He'd do rundowns and turnbacks, going down to the sixth and seventh. He'd do repeats. None of this was being done....I guess the guitar players before Robert come along just picked up what their daddies had done. It was like father, like son. Robert said, to heck with father, he'd do it the way he wanted to." And yet for all of his regard for Robert's technical accomplishments, which, while undoubtedly real, could very likely have been duplicated by any number of guitar adepts, even Johnny Shines recognizes that the real uniqueness of his music lay in its emotional appeal.

"He was a guy," Johnny wrote in his own reminiscence of Robert, "that could find a way to make a song sound good with a slide regardless of its contents or nature. His guitar seemed to talk—repeat and say words with him like no one else in the world could.... This sound affected most women in a way that I could never understand. One time in St. Louis we were playing one of the songs that Robert would like to play with someone once in a great while, 'Come On In My Kitchen.` He was playing very slow and passionately, and when we had quit, I noticed no one was saying anything. Then I realized they were crying—both women and men."

His voice, too, served as the ideal emotional conveyance. Not as heavy as House's or Muddy Waters's, for example, nor as forceful as Johnny Shines's, Robert Johnson's voice possessed a plasticity and an adaptability that lent itself to every variety of emotional effect. "It was not particularly strong," Johnny Shines says, "but it carried very well, he would sing loud and soft just for the effect of the song." You can hear this over and over in the recordings, which demonstrate a grasp of dynamics, a range of vocal effects that eludes attempts at electronic duplication. At times he seems virtually to be impersonating another, rougher singer, as he interjects a rough growl or aside; at other times he croons like the Bing Crosby records that he evidently admired, but with a sexual intensity that makes it seem as if he is crooning obscenities. What makes his work so unrepeatable is the way in which he intermixes all his approaches. At times his voice cracks, as if it really were slipping out of control; often he employs a tight, constricted vocal tone that effectively conveys this same tension. In one song he sings, "I been stuttering, oh-oh d-drive, oh oh d-drive my blues away." Occasionally you will hear a more full-throated vocal. At times he seems as free as Aretha Franklin or James Brown at their best, at other times as controlled as the most metronomic blues singer. Always, it seems, he is searching for a conscious effect.

Perhaps this very facility, this openness to new sounds and experimentation, would have led to a new kind of fusion music in the forties and fifties. Johnny Shines is convinced of it. "Robert's material was way ahead of his time," says Shines. "He was already trying to play jazz, you see, diminished sixths, diminished sevenths, all that kind of stuff that you *still* won't hear today. A lot of people think that if Robert was around today he'd still be playing the same thing, but he was playing stuff then that they're only catching up to now. If he was around today, you can't *imagine* what he'd be doing." Shines envisions a kind of Wes Montgomery progression, or perhaps something close to what Robert Jr. Lockwood plays today—a mix of swing, bebop and traditional blues—and perhaps this would have been the case. Or perhaps, like some of the less fortunate blues singers rediscovered in the sixties, in middle age he would have lost the edge off his singing voice, his playing would have become clumsy and conventional, and he would have appeared a sad reminder, a near-parody of the great artist he once had been. Unlike Shines and Lockwood he may not have been stable enough to have survived the rigors and dislocations of meeting a whole new audience which knew nothing, save what it had read, of the background of his music. And yet in the end none of this speculation really matters, for Robert Johnson, like Housman's athlete, like Orpheus, Keats, and James Dean, was kissed by the flame of youth and never lived to see the effects of the infatuation wear off.

The news of his death hit the blues community hard. Shines heard of it from Sonny Boy Williamson (Rice Miller), who claimed that Johnson had died in his arms. Son House obviously saw it as an inevitable denouement for a protege who simply would not take good advice. Robert Jr. Lockwood gave up playing the guitar for a long time because he was so affected and "because I didn't know nothing else but his songs to play." And yet the songs were kept alive, in many cases by musicians who had only casually known Robert Johnson or—in the case of Muddy Waters—known *of* Johnson. Did they speak of him? I ask Robert Jr. and Johnny Shines. When they sang his songs, did they unconsciously nod toward his memory? Did friends ever get together in the course of an evening and exchange reminiscences? "Some did, some didn't," Shines says, but, from what he and Robert say, for the most part they didn't. Robert Johnson's music was an unacknowledged presence in the lives of a whole generation of Mississippi-born musicians. They in turn passed it on to the world. Robert Jr. Lockwood recorded "Dust My Broom" for Mercury in November 1951, several months before Elmore James, another of Johnson's disciples, had a national hit with the same song (with Sonny Boy Williamson accompanying him on harmonica) on the Trumpet label. Johnny Shines did an unreleased session for Columbia in 1946 which featured several songs very much in the Robert Johnson tradition. Baby Boy Warren, who knew Johnson in Memphis, recorded "Stop Breakin' Down" around 1954, though a good part of the inspiration may have come from the first Sonny Boy Williamson's well-known adaptation. Honeyboy Edwards, along with a whole raft of others, recorded "Sweet Home Chicago" in 1952 or 1953 and continued to mine the vein of Robert Johnson material available to him. And, of course, Muddy Waters, through his popular Chess recordings, constantly drew upon the inspiration, ("Mean Red Spider," "Streamline Woman") and repertoire ("Walkin' Blues," "Kind Hearted Woman") of Robert Johnson.

Just how unaware this school of blues singers, in touch with each other yet only tangentially, was of the massive interest building in the outside world is indicated by the response of Calvin Frazier, Johnny Shines's cousin (with whom Shines and Johnson traveled to Detroit and broadcast on the Elder Moten Hour in 1937-38), when collector George Paulus found him still living in Detroit in the late sixties. "Did you ever hear of Robert Johnson?" Frazier asked Paulus then. "Calvin's description of Robert," Paulus wrote, "was of a man who was moody and quickly changing emotions. Robert, he said, was crazy, because he was so involved with music.... Calvin said he never heard any of Robert's records, so on a following visit I brought along an LP. 'Motherfucker . . . that Robert!' Calvin explained, as the disc played on, he did not even know there was an LP of a little-known figure like Johnson. He said he did not imagine I had ever known about Johnson; so he thought he would tell me about his favorite musician."

Like Joe Hill, in a sense, Robert Johnson never died; he simply became an idea. Robert Jr. Lockwood had one last flash of Johnson after his death. He was playing in Handy Park in Memphis one day probably a couple of years after Johnson had died, and a man walked up to him "and stood and just looked at me play and just stood there, and I knew he must have been doing that, you know, from some sort of concern. So finally I stopped playing, and he said, 'You're Robert Jr., aren't you?' I said, 'Yes.' He said, 'I live right around the corner. Would you go home with me? I got something I want to show you.' Well, I told him, 'Yeah,' and I walked around there, and he reached in the closet and got out a guitar. It was a Kalamazoo, big round-hole, made by Gibson. He said, 'You know this guitar?' I said, 'Yeah. It look like Robert's.' He said, 'It is.' And he told me he was one of Robert's brothers. I took the guitar and set down and played it and handed it back to him. I ain't seen him since."

Pieces of a puzzle, tantalizing clues—perhaps someday music historian Mack McCormick's long-awaited *Biography of a Phantom* will elucidate the mystery, but the title alone seems to belie this intent. It could provide more facts, certainly, supply more anecdotes, and fill out our picture of the times, but the central mystery of Robert Johnson will remain. For McCormick sees, too, a figure of intriguing illusion and common clay, the most prosaic fact and symbolic fiction, a man who, as Calvin Frazier and others have suggested, was consumed by his art but no more or less consumed than the middle-class poets, painters, filmmakers who seem so much more familiar to us today.

Not even the pictures, which McCormick first uncovered in 1972 and which almost twenty years later became common currency (one even became a stamp) in their formal and informal portraits of the blue singer as a young man, speak in an undiluted voice. These in a sense were the grail; for so long they seemed as if they must be some sort of Rosetta stone, the final verification that there was indeed a Robert Johnson who existed in the flesh and was not a construct of some collector fantasist's imagination. At the time of our original meeting, in 1976, McCormick shows me four pictures (I will not see the fifth, the now-familiar formal image of Robert Johnson with fedora and guitar, until a couple of years later). Before he will explain the pictures to me, McCormick puts me through a kind of catechism, asking me to elucidate on my perceptions of each unidentified photograph that I study searching for clues. I survey the faces, trying to read into them aspects of the story that I already know or that McCormick has just told me. Yes, McCormick confirms, that is Julia, Robert's mother, eyes half-closed, Sunday-go-to-meeting hat perched firmly atop her head, feet planted solidly on the ground, looking every inch the iron-willed matriarch. Yes, it's possible to imagine her answering the telephone in some hot little Delta town only to hear that her youngest son is dead. It's more difficult to imagine her moving from labor camp to labor camp or to get a sense of her fall, from the property-owning wife of Charles Dodds to the disgraced mistress of Noah Johnson, who may have been the most enterprising of men but who is always described somewhat dismissively, like Robert Johnson's stepfather, Dusty Willis, as a "fieldhand."

The next picture is of Robert's brother, Charles Leroy, looking sharp and dapper in a creased hat, jacket, and tie, legs crossed languidly, much like the studio shot of Robert, cradling a guitar that his brother might have played. There is a woman beside him in the picture, evidently his wife, wearing a coat and hat herself, looking pretty and expectant.

The next photograph shows a young man in a sailor's uniform, obviously pleased, obviously proud, with another man, very slightly older, standing beside him, his arm draped affectionately around the sailor's shoulder. The sailor, Mack McCormick tells me, is Robert's nephew, Louis, at home in Memphis, on his first leave from the Navy base in Norfolk, where he was stationed in 1936-37. Later he would be transferred up to Annapolis, and that was how his mother Carrie and his aunt Bessie would eventually move up to the Maryland area, where McCormick found them. Louis was very close to his uncle, and in fact, when McCormick visited Carrie in 1972, was so disturbed by the conversation that he retreated into his room and refused to come out.

And the other man in the picture? The man in the sharp pin-striped suit? That, of course, is Robert Johnson. I stare and stare at the picture, study it, scrutinize it, seek to memorize it, and for my very efforts am defeated. What is there in this face, this expression; what can you read into a photograph? The man has short nappy hair; he is slight, one foot is raised, and he is up on his toes as though stretching for height. There is a sharp crease in his pants, and a handkerchief protrudes from his breast pocket—real or imaginary, I'm no longer sure; perhaps it would be more accurate to say that the *image* of a handkerchief protrudes. His eyes are deep-set, reserved, his expression forms a half-smile, there seems to be a gentleness about him, his fingers are extraordinarily long and delicate, his head is tilted to one side. That is all. There may well be more, but that is all I can remember. I try to combine this with what I know of Johnson, what McCormick has told me. I read volumes into his relationship with Louis and imagine Louis coming home from Mississippi with his uncle's guitar. Johnny Shines's description to John Earl of Johnson himself comes to mind. "His shoulders were carried high with a little pitch forward. His sharp, slender fingers fluttered like a trapped bird.... The cataract in his left eye was immediately noticeable to anyone...." I look at the photo again and try to imagine the warmth and magnetism of the man, but in the end I am not really sure if anything is revealed.

There is a final picture, of a man dressed in khakis, looking very much like Robert Johnson, but too old, too contemporary. I ask McCormick about this picture. This, he explains, is Robert Johnson's son, one of a number of children whom McCormick found and interviewed. He was thirty-nine when the picture was taken in 1970, a businessman in a rural community, whose mother—sixteen at the time of his birth—moved in with an aunt after Robert moved on. The expression on his face is identical to that of his father, except that there does not seem to be that hint of disturbance about the eyes. Gentleness, reserve, hurt perhaps—but not the glint of pain. For him and for all of Robert Johnson's heirs—legal, not musical or spiritual—the question of Johnson's rediscovery seems not so much an artistic as a practical matter, perhaps a proud, perhaps a painful reminder of another time, another age, raising only the question that was voiced to McCormick: "Is there anything coming from my daddy's records?" For them the real Robert Johnson exists lodged firmly in memory. For the rest of us he remains to be invented.

birney imes (b.1951), *Turk's Place, Leflore County, 1989, 1989*

allison nowlin (b.1973), *New Orleans*, 1997

larry e. mcpherson (b.1943), *48 South Front, 60 South Front, NBC, Memphis,* 1999

james perry walker (b.1945), *Gathering Eggs,* 1979

peter sekaer (1901-1950), *Untitled, (Cow and Chicken Painted on Wall)*, c. 1935

henri cartier-bresson (b.1908), *Mississippi, 1962*

arthur rothstein (1914-1985), *Eddie Mitchell, Unemployed Youth, Birmingham, Alabama, 1940*

florestine perrault collins (1895-1988), *Mae Fuller Keller,* n.d.

alfred eisenstaedt (1898-1995), *Street Evangelist Preaching to the Chattanooga News Building Across the Street, Chattanooga, TN (from "A Southerner Discovers the South")*, 1938

e. j. bellocq (1873-1949), *New Orleans,* c. 1911-1913

alain desvergnes (b.1931), (series on) "YOKNAPATAWPHA" 1963-1965 The World of Faulkner, 1964

mark steinmetz (b.1961), *Athens, Georgia,1996,1996*

ashley t. mitchell (b.1973), Untitled (Woman with Vegetables, Olive Branch, MS), 1998

edward weston (1886-1958), *On Route U.S. 61, Mississippi, 1941*

george barnard (1819-1902), *Atlanta, GA, The Shell-Damaged Potter House*, 1864

ernest withers (b.1922), *Boarding House Bathroom From Which James Earl Ray Shot Dr.King, 422 South Main Street, Memphis, April1968*

deborah willis kennedy

"When people hear "the blues" they immediately conjure an image of an old black man in the country, playing the guitar (or harmonica) and singing a melancholy ditty about hard times, a lost love, or some other misfortune. Or they flash to Chicago, Memphis, or Harlem in the 1920s and imagine a full-voiced black woman, hands on hips, who sings a more upbeat song of comparable concerns. Or they imagine no one in particular, but equate the music to an emotional state: part euphoria, part doldrums, all heart and guts".
-Richard J. Powell

The blues is a life and death struggle. The blues permits the living to defend life/living. When the invitation came to contribute to this volume, I immediately began to conjure up the images described in the epigraph by art historian Richard Powell. I thought about the myriad of images I would write about and impose my own notion of visualizing the blues through the photographic images of juke joints, dancers, singers, and laborers. As I waited for sample images I struggled with what images I would write about. I thought about August Wilson's plays and wanted to use his stories to shape my essay on visualizing the blues. Later that week, I received the list of photographers who were selected for the exhibition and then considered focusing my essay on the images of the black photographers in the exhibition, as I had just completed research on a book on this subject. As it happened, I did not receive the photographic images of the "blues" as I imagined the "blues" to be. As I studied the images, I became more and more interested in contrasting my notions of the blues with the eyes of the curator. I struggled to write ... I struggled to write: how was I to decenter this construction of the blues from the music I listened to most of my life. The photographs I selected to write about were made by Gordon Parks and Ernest Withers, two image-makers who were part of my visual history. I knew their work; they were my mentors. I understood the power of their imagery and the effect their images had on contemporary society. How was I to do justice to their images in the exhibition when the images did not fit my perceptions of the blues? I began to question the social construction of the "blues" and my understanding of it. My initial response to accepting the invitation was indeed in question. This led me to look beyond the cultural symbols and media representation of the blues and reread the images through the lens of the socio-political and racial hostility, not to imply that this does not exist in the music of the blues. As I began to think about the political consciousness of these photographers and the framing of these images, I created an alternative reading of the "blues" based on racist and political events realized in the images. These photographers were not seeking to frame the discourse of the blues in their work; their photographs situated the "blues" in spatial relations of home and community. As a result, their photographs established the paradigm of visualizing the blues: confrontation/protection; power/disem-power; poor/rich; discrimination/integration; love/hate.

Beginning immediately after World War I, a large number of black Americans worked as itinerant preachers, porters, tenant farmers, factory and domestic workers throughout the rural South. Some moved to urban centers in the North and Mid-west. Documenting family activities as well as the faces of young children was an important pasttime for many black Americans. With this new migration, more and more men and women experienced racial discrimination, physical and emotional abuses, economic rejection and death. Family and community life were important to these people. Protecting the family was paramount. Many families such as the family photographed by Gordon Parks experienced episodes of hostile confrontation which intensified during the years of the modern civil rights movement. This changing attitude was captured most evocatively through the photographic medium. Memphis-born photographer Ernest Withers (b. 1922) actively fought to visualize the movement in many ways. He published and distributed a pamphlet on the murder trial of young Emmett Till, titled *Complete Photo Story of Till Murder Case.* This act revealed Withers' concern for preserving the memory of this horrific experience. He wrote in the circular, "...we are not only depicting the plight of an individual Negro, but rather of life as it affects all Negroes in the United States....In brief we are presenting this photo story not in an attempt to stir up racial animosities or to question the verdict in the Till Murder Case, but in the hope that this booklet might serve to help our nation dedicate itself to seeing that such incidents need not occur again." Photo curator, Brooks Johnson describes Withers in this manner: "He is unquestionably one of the most significant photographers of the [civil rights] movement and Withers was there not only to document the struggle but also to work actively to propel the movement forward."

Through text and images, black photographers, artists and intellectuals expressed their frustrations and exposed the injustices their communities experienced. They reflected and represented the dreams and ideals of the black working class and underclass by making socially relevant and class-conscious images of the African-American community.

As early as the 1930s and 1940s, photographers began working as photojournalists for the black press and national periodicals such as *Our World, Ebony, Jet, Sepia,* and *Flash*, magazines marketed to African-American readers.   The period following World War II saw a more comprehensive coverage of political events and public protests. What made this feasible was the introduction of smaller handheld cameras and major magazines such as *LOOK* and *LIFE* which aided photographers in expressing their frustration and discontentment with social conditions and political inequality.

On June 19, 1963, a civil rights bill was introduced in the U. S. Senate, seven days after the murder of NAACP leader Medgar Evers in Jackson, Mississippi. Not surprisingly,1963 was a pivotal year for a larger number of black photographers. Throughout the country men, women, and young people were organizing busloads of people who were planning to attend the March on Washington. With unmistakable compassion and a keen sense of composition, numerous photographers captured the events of the period. Withers' photograph *National Guard Helicopter and Troops Prepare to Take James Meredith to University of Mississippi from Millington Naval Base* was made in 1963. It captures black and white troops in a fixed position, one black trooper stares defiantly into the camera while another looks as if he is questioning their position. The white troopers appear to be disengaged.

By the early 1960s, the civil rights movement had become a national crusade for human rights for all oppressed people. Newspapers and magazines throughout the world had published gripping images of racial hatred in Birmingham, in the greatest outpouring of universal sentiment since the days of abolitionists, over one hundred years before.   The most brutalizing events caused photographers to speak out en masse. Images that convincingly told the story and the activities of the modern civil rights movement were well documented by black photographers in this country. During the most active years of the civil rights, black power and black arts movements, a period that began in the early 1960s, a significant number of socially committed men and women became photographers. They set a different standard in documenting the struggles, achievements and tragedies of the freedom movement by focusing on their own communities.

Ernest C. Withers began photographing at the age of fourteen. For more than twenty-five years, he maintained a studio on Beale Street, also known as the "Main Street of Negro America." His photographs document activities of civil rights workers, musicians and itinerant preachers. Significant within his large body of work is his ability to document the duality of life in this southern town: there are Jim Crow signs (colored only) that are juxtaposed with images of white evangelists preaching to all black congregations; then there is a photograph of blues singer B.B. King with Elvis Presley posing in oversized tuxedos. Such photographs offer a view of Withers's community as he knew it. As he writes:

"Photography is a collection of memories . . . . When I go through the negatives with various images out of the past, it has a tendency to jog my mind. The average person who doesn't go through such images doesn't have their minds [sic] as refreshed about the past. It renews your memory. It starts you to thinking retrospectively. . . . In my Civil Rights photographs, I want people to see the conditions of the times. I want them to be a reflection of what transpired."

Kansas native, Gordon Parks (b.1912), invites the viewer not to simply accept the experiences of his subjects; he requires the viewer to become a participant in understanding his subjects' conditions through visual empathy. Through these photographs we are able to see the photographer Parks as the man behind the camera. He is a man who is increasingly committed to his photographic work—a work he uses to combat poverty and racism. This undaunting commitment permitted him to transform his own life at an early age and to become one of America's most important photographers. He saw art not only as poignant rendering but also as political.

The importance of Parks photography in the genre of documentary photography is surely beyond question. His photographic images provided his audience with a broader reading of the African American people. He contributed to a transformation of the reading of African American photographic images in his *LIFE* photography and thereby allowed the wider American public to consider more humanistic aspects of the people he photographed and their struggle for daily survival. It is Parks's own documentation and analysis of the historical struggles of black people that authenticate his photographs.

Central to experiencing Parks's imagery is the sense of memory and how memory plays in looking at his photographs. Parks seems to be constantly mediating between the beauty of art and the realism of documentary photography. Through photographs Parks' visually interrogated the imbalance of the working poor. He encountered poverty, despair and hope within the same frame.

Parks's photographs allow the contemporary reader to analyze these experiences within the context of the segregated South. The photography of the Willie Causey Family also positions Parks in the continuum of visualizing the blues in American culture. He writes, "Looking back now to the black revolution of the 1960s, I realize why we refused to wait for justice any longer–especially from the Supreme Court. Only after a long struggle did it outlaw school segregation, but even then black children would still be harassed by white mobs before entering school. Even then Federal troops had to be brought in to escort them to their desks, while 'Lynch 'em!' thundered through the corridors. When Rosa Parks was jailed for not giving her seat to a white man on an Alabama bus, the sit-ins would arrive. As one group wiped away blood and spit, another one walked in to suffer more blood and spit. When the Freedom Riders began their terror-filled forays into the deepest South, their buses were firebombed, their windows smashed, tires slashed, and their young Riders beaten. A bomb exploded inside a Birmingham church and four black children died. In Mississippi a white Southerner aimed his gun at the back of Medgar Evers, the civil rights leader, and hit his mark. White police waited with clubs, guns, water hoses, and dogs to wreak havoc on his mourners. But armed only without blackness against this violence, we would keep marching on".

Gordon Parks and Ernest Withers' photographs resonate with emotion. The dingy bathroom in *Boarding House Bathroom From Which James Earl Ray Shot Dr. King, 422 South Main Street, Memphis, April 1968*, captured by Withers eerily depicts the sadness and loss I imagine he felt when he encountered this space. Parks and Withers' words and images helped to resituate my understanding of visualizing the blues as they describe the experiences of prejudice, discrimination and racism. Their words express the outrage of the dominant voices of the movement– men, women and children who resented racism and willingly rebelled and dared to question. Their work is a testimony to the depth of understanding the legacy of the blues.

jane rule burdine (b.1946), *Elizabeth Says Goodbye, Greenville, Mississippi, 1993*

nicholas nixon (b.1947), *Yazoo City, Mississippi, 1979*

lee friedlander (b.1934), *New Orleans 1970, 1970*

doris ulmann (1882-1934), *Mr. Ritchie, Viper, KY, c. 1933*

walker evans (1903-1975), *Kitchen Wall, Alabama Farmstead*, 1936

huger foote (b.1961), *Jeni-Su,* 1995

jack delano (b.1914), *Convicts in the County Jail. Greene County, Georgia, June,1941*

p.h. polk (1898-1984), *Freedom Dance*, 1965

david julian leonard (b.1962), *Payne's Bar B Q, 1995*

guenevere taft (b.1972), *"Liquor Store Series, Off of I-40, West Memphis, Arkansas,"* 1999

alexander gardner (1821-1882), *Richmond, Virginia, Ruins of the Gallego Flour Mill, April,1865*

ernest withers (b.1922), *Destruction on Beale Street, Memphis, After the Sanitation Workers' March*, March 1968

william christenberry (b.1936), *From The Klan Room ,1982*, 1982

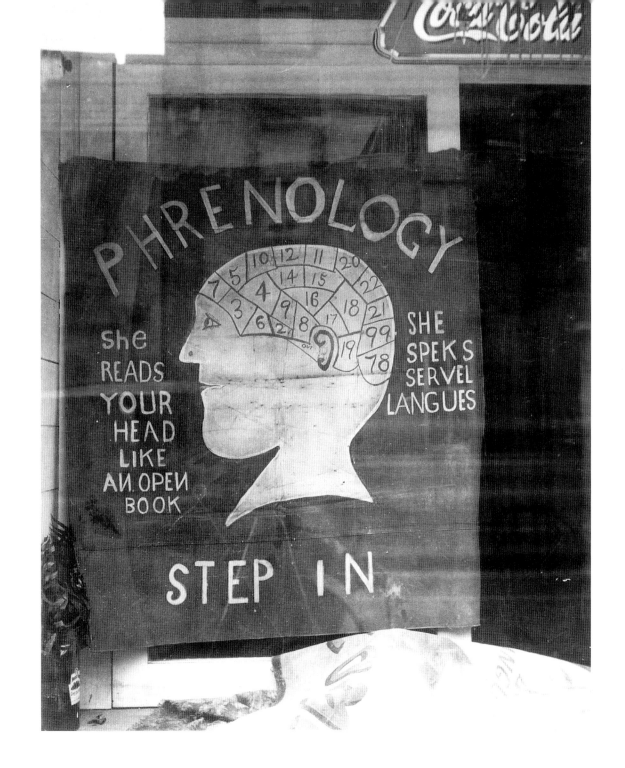

peter sekaer (1901-1950), *Phrenology*, c.1939

jack spencer (b.1951), *Happy Child, Como, Mississippi,1996*, 1996

paul buchanan (b. c.1910), *#55, from <u>The Picture Man</u>* c.1930-50

eudora welty (b.1909), *Saturday Strollers, Grenada*, 1935

jane rule burdine (b.1946), *Natchez Ladies,* 1981

william albert allard (b.1937), *Juke House, Bentonia, Mississippi, 1997*

deborah luster (b.1951), *Young Rappers,* 1993

mark steinmetz (b.1961), *New Orleans, 1995*, 1995

birney imes (b. 1951), *Bell's Place, 1984*

bill wyman

I was born in South East London, at Lewisham Hospital on October 24th 1936. After the usual few days in Hospital my Mother took me home to a tiny house in Lower Sydenham. It was a long way from the Delta.

A month either side of my birthday musicians from the South were recording the Blues. Little Brother Montgomery and Walter Vinson in New Orleans, Washboard Sam, Johnnie Temple and Memphis Minnie were all recording in Chicago. The Devil's Son in Law, Peetie Wheatstraw, was in Chicago along with Kokomo Arnold cutting five sides. Two days later Big Bill Broonzy was also in the Windy City. Then just a month after I was born, Robert Johnson was in a hotel room in San Antonio recording his first records.

I was blissfully unaware of all this activity, and it would be over twenty years before I even heard their names. Growing up in London during the war was an experience that I'll never forget; my Dad was discharged from the army in 1946, by which time my two younger brothers, two sisters and I were living in a small house in Penge. This was one of the poorest parts of Southeast London and we were no better off than most of our neighbours. Our house had no heating, no bathroom, and the toilet was in the garden. We had gas lighting. For our weekly bath my mum boiled water while I took a large zinc bath off the back-garden wall and placed it in the kitchen, where we filled it with water. Starting with the youngest, we bathed in turn, washing our hair with a large slab of soap. Being the eldest meant that I had the filthy water; I got out dirtier than I got in. I then had to dry myself with the same towel that the others had used. Our whole family shared one toothbrush and we all suffered bad teeth. Toothpaste was expensive, so we used salt. New clothes were rare - everything was handed down. We each wore one pair of socks a week, changing on Sundays; they almost stood beside our beds at night! We were poor. In no way would I compare my upbringing to what black families in the Delta had to face, but it was tough. One reason, perhaps, why I found myself relating so strongly, many years later, to the feelings and attitudes inspired by the Blues.

In 1955 I joined the Royal Air Force and was shipped off to Germany. Musically it was the making of me. I got to listen to American Forces Military Radio. I woke up to country music, a programme called "The Stick Buddy Jamboree". It was the beginnings of Rock & Roll; I was listening to Elvis, Bill Haley, Fats Domino and Little Richard for the first time: Great records that you could not even hear, let alone buy in Britain. In 1957 I was home on leave and went to a Cinema with a few friends to see a film called "Rock Rock Rock". First there was the Johnny Burnette Trio, then suddenly on came Chuck Berry. I had never seen Chuck; I had only heard him on radio. He was wearing that white suit, doing his pigeon toe thing, playing that little Gibson Les Paul guitar and singing "You Can't Catch Me". The hairs went up on the back of my neck for the first time ever in my life, I was in shock, this was it! The rest of the audience was roaring with laughter and I'm sitting there thinking this is the greatest thing that's ever happened to me. Later I found out this is how Brian Jones felt the first time he heard Elmore James; he said that the earth moved.

I started to write to America to order Chuck's records. On my return to Germany some of the other guys in the camp and I formed a Skiffle group. Some years later I found out that in 1929 Blind Lemon Jefferson and other stars of the Paramount label made a record entitled Hometown Skiffle. In Britain Skiffle became all the rage in the 50s as a result of Lonnie Donegan. They got the name from that record. It was through Skiffle that many British bands got their start: The Who, Led Zeppelin, The Beatles and The Stones we all started off playing it.

When I finished my military service I formed a group called the Cliftons in Southeast London. Then in 1962 I joined the Stones. My interest in the Blues soon became a passion. Brian loved Elmore James, and all of us loved the music of Jimmy Reed, Bo Diddley, Chuck Berry and of course Muddy Waters. It was Brian who chose our name from Muddy's song; Brian gave us our early Blues education. There is no question that the influence of Chuck and Bo helped to mould our sound, to make us what we were. The first time we went into a recording studio together was on 11th. March 1963. With a very young producer, Glyn Johns, we cut Bo Diddley's "Road Runner" and "Diddley Daddy", Muddy Waters "I Want To Be Loved" and Jimmy Reed's "Honey What's Wrong". We had 5 minutes left and did a quick take on Jimmy's "Bright Lights Big City".

Well you all know the rest; playing clubs, turned into cinemas, then to bigger halls, then to stadiums and outdoor festivals. Our little Blues band became what some have called the greatest rock and roll band in the world ...whatever that means! What was remarkable is how five young English guys took on board the influences of the Blues and then helped give it back to America. We pointed white middle class America towards their own, largely undiscovered, deep Blues well.

The bigger we became the more I became fascinated with where the musicians that influenced us got *their* influences. Where did Chuck Berry get his inspiration? How did Jimmy Reed learn his craft? Who taught Muddy? I became a detective. Touring the world gave me the opportunity to seek out old Blues records. In America, especially in Chicago, Ian Stewart and I would go in search of little old record stores where we thought we might find something interesting. We usually did. I have collected thousands of Blues record and CDs, the work of just about every Blues artist that has ever recorded. I became particularly fascinated by pre - war blues, growing to love Charley Patton, Blind Blake, Bo Carter, Ethel Waters, Son House, Blind Willie McTell, Blind Willie Johnson, Skip James, Tommy & Robert Johnson, Memphis Minnie, Papa Charlie Jackson how long have you got? I even found out about the Devil's Son in Law who recorded just two days after I was born.

During my musical career I have been lucky enough to play with Muddy, the Wolf, Buddy Guy, Junior Wells, and Eric Clapton to name just a few; I have learned the Blues from all of them. Once I was asked if white men can play the Blues. My answer? Yes, if they really try hard enough. I'm still trying, still learning, still loving the Blues; my friend and member of my band, The Rhythm Kings, Georgie Fame said to me once "The Blues are America's greatest art form of the 20th Century". He's not wrong!

Let the Blues Odyssey continue.

tseng kwong chi (1950-1990), *Graceland, Tennessee, 1979, 1979*

patty carroll (b.1946), *Sun Studio, Memphis, 1994*

danny lyon (b. 1942), *The Movement, 1964*, 1964

andres serrano (b.1950), *Klanswoman (Grand Klaliff II)*, 1990

mathew brady (c.1823-1896), *Quarters of Men in Fort Sedwick Known as Fort Hell before Petersburg, "Civil War: Brady's Gallery Album Folder #1," 1863*

walker evans (1903-1975), *Negro Houses, Atlanta, GA, 1936*

lewis wickes hine (1874-1940), *Girls at Work in Textile Mill from Child Labor (Textiles) series, c. 1912*

mike disfarmer (1884-1959), *Untitled*, c.1940s

marion post wolcott   (1910-1990), *Gambling with their "Cotton Money" in Back of a Juke Joint, Clarksdale Mississippi, 1939*

marion post wolcott   (1910-1990), *Negroes Jitterbugging in a Juke Joint, Clarksdale, Mississippi, 1939*

peter sekaer (1901-1950), *Mardi Gras Audience, c.1939*

whit griffin (b.1980), *Recluse,* 1999

lindsay brice (b.1957), *Bedroom Mantle, Summer, 1998*

mike smith (b.1951), *Cash Hollow, TN, 1999*

jeane umbreit (b.1953), *In Observance of Front Porch Etiquette,* 1988

lee friedlander (b.1934), *Memphis, TN,1973*, 1973

jonathan postal, *Wedding, New Orleans,* n.d.

ralston crawford (1906-1978), *New Orleans*, 1961

willam eggleston (b.1939), *Greenville, Mississippi, c.1986*

milly moorhead (b.1949), *Too Much Saturday Night, c.* 1988

allison nowlin (b.1973), *New Orleans, 1996*

alain desvergnes (b.1931), (series on) "YOKNAPATAWPHA" 1963-1965 The World of Faulkner, 1963

jane rule burdine (b. 1946), *Curtain, Lafayette County, Mississippi, 1972*

charles reagan wilson

In *One Writer's Beginnings*, Eudora Welty gives a superb portrait of the creativity nurtured in her by her family and community in Mississippi. Her parents embodied a creative dialogue. Her father's creativity was in technology–the telescopes around the house to look at the moon and stars, the clocks that taught her the importance of time, the Kodak camera that gave her a visceral sense of imagery. Her father's creativity with such things looked toward the future, toward the progress to which creative inventions could lead. Welty's mother's creative gifts were different ones. She loved books, reading, and artistic beauty. Every room in her home was one in which young Eudora could hear stories read from books, books for which her parents scrimped and saved. Her mother sang to her, resulting in Welty developing an inner voice, so that when she read, she heard a voice. Her mother sent her to preschoool art classes, where she learned to associate the smell of flowers with the pictures she drew.

Fannie, the black sewing lady, came around weekly, and young Welty heard from her stories: stories of black people and white people, of good people and bad people, of gossip, rumor, wild exaggeration, and truth. Conversation was a simple daily art but an important one. A friend of Welty's mother would go with them on Sunday afternoons for a ride. "My mother sat in the back with her friend," Welty writes, "and I'm told that as a small child I would ask to sit in the middle, and say as we started off,'Now talk'."

Eudora Welty, of course, is one of the premier embodiments of creativity in the American South, and her reflections suggest some of the forces behind the different kinds of creativity that existed there–the role of parents, the creativity often associated with men and women, the folk culture of storytelling and conversation, the role of institutions like art classes, the importance of books, the centrality of individuals who serve as teachers. Welty is certainly not typical, but she is prime evidence of the South as fertile ground for the creative spirit.

One might gain a different picture of creativity in wondering about the origin of the blues. After all, it was working class music. Delta blues performer Bukka White once noted that the blues started "back across them fields . . . right behind one of them mules or one of them log houses, one of them log camps or the levee camp. That's where the blues sprung from." Mississippi bluesman Eddie "Son" House agreed. "People wonder a lot about where the blues came from. Well, when I was coming up, people did more singing in the fields than they did anywhere else." Folklorist David Evans concludes that near the end of the nineteenth century, the vocal expressions of traditional Southern black field hollers "were set to instrumental accompaniment and given a musical structure, an expanded range of subject matter and a new social context" that gave birth to the blues. The field hollers had been vernacular, group music among African Americans on farms and plantations, but the blues especially encouraged creativity among performers, who worked for individuality of expression and timeliness, as well as drawing from oral tradition. The emergence of this new creativity in the blues in the 1890's was surely directly related to the social context, as the first generation of African Americans born under freedom came to maturity. Their extraordinary musical innovations would include not only the blues, but the cakewalk, jazz, ragtime, barbershop quartet singing, and gospel music.

What is creativity and how is it related to the broader culture in which creative people, whether writers or musicans or others, live? Creativity is bringing something new into existence. The most honored individuals make the big leaps—the Charley Patton who defined a new art form, the blues, out of the folk ingredients of African American music in the Delta; or the William Faulkner who took the stock characters of earlier Southern literature and more deeply than anyone before explored their humanity. The modern world often sees creativity in terms of psychology, identifying such personal qualities as intelligence, spontaneity, originality, or sincerity. Some individuals are so wild and unorthodox in their creativity that we naturally think of "genius," and the South has surely produced those spirits. But the deeper question raised in the region's cultural history is how a place with so many apparent social problems has still nurtured a deep creativity in many of its people. How do we bring together the social context with individual creativity? A social focus on creativity points toward the culture of the South, with creativity not just the result of individual genius but emerging from a social context that encouraged certain kinds of creativity while perhaps discouraging other. The cultural base set the parameters for individual achievements.

Looking at the twentieth-century South and considering what are generally regarded as the region's highest cultural achievements, I want to argue that this creativity resulted from the long dominance of a traditional culture and the stimulus the Southern environment and social system have provided to individuals who have generated creative sparks. The modernization of the region itself became the final spark that galvinized the creative spirit for many artists.

If we had considered this issue in the early twentieth century, though, the South would have seemed an unlikely spot to even think about the possibility of high cultural achievement. H.L. Mencken, the liveliest critic of the region's culture, complained in the 1920s of the cultural barrenness he saw in the region. He claimed that classical musicians, symphonies, ballets, and good poets were hard to find south of the Mason-Dixon line. He blamed this sorry state of affairs on the region's decline since antebellum times, the rurality of the South, and the religious orthodoxy that stifled innovation. He saw no arts in the South except "the lower reaches of the gospel hymn." Mencken was witty indeed and he had a point. He might also have mentioned the poverty that blanketed the region after the Civil War. As late as the 1930s, the federal government proclaimed the South "the nation's No. 1 economic problem." The lack of funding available for formal cultural institutions meant that the region did have fewer symphonies and ballets and also fewer libraries and good universities and schools than in other parts of the nation. A weak infrastructure inadequately supported certain kinds of creative and intellectual life.

The predominantly rural nature of life in the South meant that the region lacked big cities, which have been associated with nurturing innovative cultural achievements since the classical age of Greece and Rome. London, Paris, and New York City have been the cultural capitals of the modern era, at least in most high cultural matters. And then, of course, people still puzzle over how a region with such a high illiteracy rate produced all those writers; "there are more people who write novels down there than can read them" is a familiar saying. In a predominantly rural, agrarian society, illiteracy did not prevent you from learning traditional practical skills, but it did hamper certain kinds of creativity because it meant a population less capable than otherwise of utilizing written knowledge and the innovations that come from that information.

Racial obsessions haunted the South of Mencken's day, another restriction on creative spirits. Richard Wright pondered how he became a writer living in the "southern darkness" of Jim Crow segregation. "The external world of whites and blacks," he wrote, "which was the only world that I had ever known, surely had not evoked in me any belief in myself." He realized that he existed "emotionally on the sheer, thin margin of Southern culture," experiencing dreadfully the obstacle of racial categorization. Whites, and blacks too, told him he could not aspire to the highest cultural realms.

These obstacles were mighty ones, tragic burdens for many of the South's people. And yet Wright went on to become a literary giant, part of the flowering of creativity in the Southern Literary Renaissance after 1920. Mississippi, which had earlier been the birthplace of the blues, became one center of the region's literary acclaim, as writers from that state alone received one Nobel Prize, eight Pulitzer Prizes for fiction, drama, and journalism, and four New York Drama Critics Awards. William Faulkner used the specifics of Southern history to embody his dramas of "the human heart in conflict with itself." Thomas Wolfe, Robert Penn Warren, Katherine Anne Porter, Ralph Ellison, Carson McCullers, and Tennesseee Williams are only a few representatives of the accomplished literary culture of the modern South. They typically came out of middle class backgrounds and were often university educated and well traveled. They had grown up in a South that for two generations had lived with the dislocations and turbulence of Confederate defeat, which stimulated their art to new heights. Their themes of agrarian life, the memory of the Old South and the Civil War, religious values, the tensions of the biracial society, and the modernization of society were epitomized in *I'll Take My Stand* (1930), a polemical statement made at the beginning of the Southern Literary Renaissance.

When we think about the folk and popular musicians who emerged in the twentieth-century South, we need to broaden the idea of a Southern Literary Renaissance to a Southern Cultural Renaissance in the same midcentury years. Whether the blues music of Robert Johnson, Muddy Waters, and Blind Lemon Jefferson; the country music of Roy Acuff, Jimmie Rodgers, and Hank Williams; the jazz of Louis Armstrong, Lester Young, and Thelonious Monk; or the early rock of Elvis Presley, Little Richard, and Fats Domino–the South fostered a world-class musical culture. These entertainers were typically working class, often coming from very poor backgrounds and many times African American. Family and church had taught them the centrality of talking and singing to their lives, and their creativity now took them into profitable new venues. Their work displayed some but not all of the same concerns as Southern writers in those years–the memory of agrarian life, the importance of religion, and the sense of changing times was surely strong but the folk and early popular performers rarely sang of the Civil War and only black performers spoke in an idiom of overt racial concerns.

More recently still, the South is receiving recognition for its painting, sculptural, and photographic achievements. Two recent masters, William Christenberry and William Eggleston, for example, draw explicitly from the Southern cultural context and yet achieve broad artistic acclaim. Christenberry photographs in the Hale County, Alabama, that Walker Evans documented earlier, while Eggleston has captured the visual wonders of Graceland. In another example, Southern outsider artists since the 1960s, such as Howard Finster, R.A. Miller, and Lonny Holley, have come out of a rural Southern aesthetic that represents the latest phase of regional creativity rooted in the South's culture. A century from now, this art may be seen as the equal to the South's earlier literary and musical flowering, which also rested in rural traditions undergoing social change. These examples do not exhaust the list of cultural achievements, yet the point is clear that these achievements are not just individual ones but represent a cultural phenomenon.

Southern cultural creativity grew out of the region's folk traditions. Southern cohesiveness rested in an agrarian culture that had taken root in the early South, spread westward in the nineteenth century, and survived the Civil War. Southern rural and small town people knew each other, living in a face-to-face society. They gathered around the courthouse square or the country crossroads store. Crop cycles, community life, and church worship structured daily life. It was a deferential society, with a hierarchical class system rooted in differences in wealth, gender, and skin color. Orthodoxy ruled, yet it allowed for eccentricity as long as the foundations of the society were not challenged. Theorists talked of the importance of "place" to the system, and indeed, it could seem almost medieval in its stress on individuals staying within their "place" in the social order.

The relationship to the land was the central context for Southern life in the folk society that dominated the South until recently, resulting in a sense of place to which creative people responded, giving them a special focus from which to see the world. This sense of place has been central in Southern artistic life. Southern artists have lived in a place that stimulated their senses. "Let us begin by discussing the weather," wrote historian Ulrich B. Phillips in the early twentieth century in discussing Southern distinctiveness, and artists have long used the super-charged heat and humidity of the Southeast–especially the Deep South--and its sometimes exotic animals, flora, and fauna for dramatic effect. The sensory South, the world of sight and smell and sound, the efflourescense of the landscape, has stimulated not only Southerners but artists from elsewhere who have come south to paint or to take photographs.

One could embrace the sense of place that came from the South's natural world while rejecting its social meanings. Richard Wright noted that "my deepest instincts had always made me reject the 'place' to which the white South had assigned me," and yet this conviction did not prevent his appreciation of the sensory Southern place, as seen in the following passage from his memoir *Black Boy*:

There was the delight I caught in seeing long straight rows of red and green vegetables stretching away in the sun to the bright horizon.
There was the faint, cool kiss of sensuality when dew came on my cheeks and shins as I ran down the wet green garden paths in the early mornings.
There was the vague sense of the infinite as I looked down upon the yellow, dreaming waters of the Mississippi River from the verdant bluffs of Natchez.

The sense of place also rested, though, on the cultural memories of the past. Writers could look around and see customs, rituals, and ways that connected to generations of people who had lived agrarian-centered lives. Partly, this sense of place derived from a sense of history, a tangible awareness of history's impact on the South. White Southerners remembered Confederate defeat and black Southerners remembered slavery and segregation as seminal moments, past yet still alive. Partly, this sense of place had to do with family, in the ties between generations and the place of honor the elderly occupied. Alice Walker has noted this sensibility in terms of African American creativity: "What the black Southern writer inherits as a natural right is a sense of community." Her mother was "a walking history of our community," and "always, in one's memory, there remain all the rituals of one's growing up." The "daily dramas" that grew out of this agrarian-centered place "are pure gold." Writers, musicians, painters, and photographers in the South lived within a stimulating physical and social environment that promoted expressiveness.

The Southern folk culture that produced an intense sense of place was an oral culture, and the facility with language that emerged from this storytelling, conversation-oriented society was surely of central importance to nurturing creative expression. Remember Welty's story of riding between her mother and her friend and telling them to talk. Bluesman Son House saw the oral culture working through the pervasiveness of song. He recalled that black workers in the fields would sing all the time: "they'd sing about their girl friend or about almost anything–mule–anything. They'd make a song of it just to be hollering." Blues singers themselves often came from church-going families, and the songs, stories, proverbs, and sermons they heard in religious settings were also part of a culture whose features–sacred and secular–were in close proximity, within "shouting distance."

The folk culture thus bequeathed language gifts to its people, but that culture itself began to change under the impress of modernization, the economic development that produced cities, factories, and consumerism in the early twentieth-century South. One cultural result of modernization was the appearance of mass culture, beginning especially in the 1920s. Literary critics have debated the origins of the Southern Literary Renaissance, disagreeing over whether the South had modernized enough by the 1920s for literary creativity to have emerged from the awareness of social change. In fact, the South had not truly modernized in the 1920s or for decades thereafter, but creativity in some forms, such as folk and popular music, did not depend on a general economic development. With a broadened focus beyond just the literary culture, evidence surely suggests that musicians and performers knew quite tangibly times had changed, and the changes contributed to new forms of Southern creativity. The phonograph, commercial radio, and the public address system promoted the recording, marketing, and performance of Southern folk music for profit by the 1920s and early 1930s.

What was new about the cultural context of creativity in the South at that point was its movement beyond the localism of the folk culture to a broader regional and national context. This change did not at all destroy Southern creativity musically, any more than new access to Northern literary markets ended the creativity of Southern writers. Indeed, these changes, including increasing commercialization, were a spur to creativity. The South became a prime source of performers and lyrical themes for the national culture, just as its writers soon came to occupy a central stage in the American literary world. These creative people drew from earlier Southern traditions, yet gave innovative interpretations of them appropriate to the modern world.

Southern creativity brought empowerment to creative spirits who had often grown up economically disadvantaged. Historian Pete Daniel writes of the region's "lowdown culture," which in the 1950s produced a flowering of creative music through early rock 'n' roll. Sam Phillips, the founder of Sun Records in Memphis, recognized the "untamed streak" in poor white and black youth, who had recently moved from the rural South to Memphis. The middle class could not get beyond their "accent, dress, and decibel level," and these young people often violated their society's Jim Crow segregation strictures in their search for new opportunities to escape the limitations of the poverty with which they had grown up. They seized the opportunities of a South that after World War II was rapidly modernizing. Phillips nurtured the creative energy of this new Southern generation. With Elvis Presley, Phillip found what he wanted musically as a producer–"the blues with a mania." Presley, like other early Southern rock performers, found the psychological and economic success that was sometimes beyond their dreams. Phillips's phrase suggests the creative energy that led to one of the South's major cultural achievements.

Southern creativity of the twentieth century thus came out of the region's folk culture, its sense of place, its stimulating physical environment, and its facility with language. All these were brought into focus for creative spirits undergoing the uprooting traumas of modernization. Finally, though, one must reckon with another central factor–the biracial context of creativity in the South. Despite the desire of Southern whites to maintain a segregated culture, blacks and whites from early in Southern history engaged in cultural interaction. It is the story of cultural groups with distinctive ways, Europeans and Africans, who created a new culture in the South. In the course of living on Southern soil for three centuries, blacks and whites developed two societies, two cultures. But they also exchanged cultural knowledge and blended them in creative ways. Structurally they were separated, but culturally they interacted to create something new. Jimmie Rodgers heard black singers on the railroad crews of Mississippi and then created the white blues as the father of country music. Hank Williams learned to play the guitar from a black Montgomery, Alabama, street singer. Ray Charles listened to country music growing up in Georgia, so it was not surprising when he chose to record a soulful country music album in the 1960s. Elvis Presley grew up poor, in a society that threw together blacks and whites who shared economic deprivation and also their music.

Looking back on it, the Southern biracial history that produced not only the musical geniuses of the 1950s but other creative achievements as well has been a magnificent social drama, complicated in the twentieth century by Southerners moving from a traditional society into modern life. As much as any American place, the South has wrestled with deep-seated human hopes, fears, and anxieties rooted in cultural interaction and social change. Its social system has been turbulent, given to vibrant emotional displays and clear and passionate expressions. It is no wonder that the South's artists have been nurtured there: the tensions of Southern society have fed efforts to create new ways of understanding these human dramas.

bob adelman (b. 1930), *Mr. Sam "Skee" Stanford Trucking a Bale of Cotton in a Local Gin, Camden, Alabama, (From Down Home)*, 1965

arthur rothstein (1914-1985), *Eroded Land, Farm Securty Administration*, c. 1935

danny lyon (b.1942), *Talahatchie County, Mississippi*, 1964

william christenberry (b.1936), *Church across Field of Cotton, Pickinsville, Alabama1981*, 1981

w. eugene smith (1919-1978), *KKK Grandmother*, c. 1951-1958

david julian leonard (b.1962), *Hunt & Fish & Fireworks for Jesus*, 2000

birney imes (b.1951), *Bailey's Late Nite Spot, Rolling Fork, MS, 1984*

jim dow (b.1942), *Chapel at Mr. Roussel's, Vacherine, Louisiana, 1978*

william greiner (b.1957), *Color T.V. in Bayou*, 1993

huger foote (b.1961), *Untitled*, 1999

marion post wolcott   (1910-1990), *Board and Split Rail Fences Around Fields of Shocked Corn. Near Marion, Virginia, 1940*

jeane umbreit (b.1953), *Cotton Exchange, 1988*

debbie fleming caffery (b.1948), *Sleeping Lizards, 1986*

c.c. lockwood, *Flat Lake Sunset,* 1980

logan young, *Untitled, 1999*

Visualizing the Blues Exhibition Checklist

Nineteenth Century

Anonymous
Catherine Hunt, Black Slave Woman, Holding Her Mistress' Baby, Julia Hunt, 1852 tintype, in original dark brown case, 4"x 7 1/2," Collection of the Tennessee State Museum, Nashville
page 29

Anonymous
With Most of their Men Folk Away at the Front, Women Ran the Plantations During the Civil War. These Are All Slaves, 1863, 1863, copy photograph mounted to board, 6" x 6 3/8," Collection of The New -York Historical Society, New York City Negative # 73980 © Collection of The New -York Historical Society
page 37

George Barnard (1819-1902)
Atlanta GA, The Shell-Damaged Potter House, 1864, fiber base print, printed later, 10 1/2"x10 3/8," Collection of the Library of Congress, Prints and Photographs Division, Selected Civil War Photographs, 1861-1865 Collection [LC-B811-2717]
page 72

Mathew Brady (c.1823-1896)
Quarters of Men in Fort Sedwick Known as Fort Hell Before Peterburg, "Civil War: Brady's Gallery Album Folder #1," 1863, albumen print, 7 1/4"x 9 1/4," Collection of The New-York Historical Society, New York City, Negative #73981 © Collection of The New-York Historical Society
page 109

Alexander Gardner (1821-1882)
Richmond, Virginia, Ruins of the Gallego Flour Mill, April 1865, fiber base print, printed later, 10 1/2"x13 3/8," Collection of the Library of Congress Prints and Photographs Division, Selected Civil War Photographs, 1861-1865 Collection, [LC-B815-0886]
page 89

Alexander Gardner (1821-1882)
Antietam, Maryland, Confederate Dead By A Fence on Hagerstown Road, September 1862, fiber-base print, printed later 10 1/2"x13 3/8," Collection of the Library of Congress Prints and Photographs Division, Selected Civil War Photographs, 1861-1865 Collection, [LC-B8171-0560]
page 36

Twentieth Century

Bob Adleman (b. 1930)
*Mr. Sam"Skee" Stanford Trucking a Bale of Cotton in a Local Gin. Camden, Alabama, (from Down Home),*1965, black and white gelatin print, 13 x 10," Courtesy of the Artist, © Bob Adleman from *Down Home*
page 138

William Albert Allard (b.1937)
Juke House, Bentonia, Mississippi, 1997, color photograph, 23 5/8" x 19 5/8," Courtesy of National Geographic Society Image Collection, Washington, DC
page 98

E.J. Bellocq (1873 -1949)
New Orleans, c. 1911- 13, printed later by Lee Friedlander from original negative, 10"x 8," Collection of Logan Young, Memphis
page 67

E.J. Bellocq (1873 -1949)
New Orleans, c. 1911- 13, printed later by Lee Friedlander from original negative, 8"x 10," Collection of Logan Young, Memphis
Not Illustrated

Margaret Bourke-White (1904 -1971)
*Hood's Chapel, Georgia,*1936, vintage gelatin silver print, 13" x 9 5/8," Courtesy of Howard Greenberg Gallery, New York
page 35

Lindsay Brice (b. 1957)
Bedroom Mantle, Summer, 1998, cibachrome on aluminum, 16" x 23 1/4," Courtesy of the Artist
page 118

Paul Buchanan (b. c. 1910)
#55, c. 1930-50 (Description: three men standing), silver print, 4"x 2 1/2," Courtesy of Ann Hawthorne, Washington DC, from *The Picture Man*
page 95

Paul Buchanan (b. c. 1910)
#25, c. 1930-50, (Description: boy standing on the front of a car), silver print, 4"x 2 1/2," Courtesy of Ann Hawthorne, Washington DC, from *The Picture Man*
page 94

Jane Rule Burdine (b. 1946)
Natchez Ladies, 1981, c-print, 13 1/2" x 9," Courtesy of the Artist
page 97

Jane Rule Burdine (b. 1946)
Willow Run Hunting Club, Hollandale, Mississippi, 1988, c-print, 13 1/2" x 9,"
Courtesy of the Artist
page 47

Jane Rule Burdine (b. 1946)
Elizabeth Says Goodbye, Greenville, Mississippi, 1993, c-print, 9"x13 1/2,"
Courtesy of the Artist
page 79

Jane Rule Burdine (b. 1946)
Curtain, Lafayette County, Mississippi, 1972 c-print, 13 1/2" x 9 7/8," Courtesy of the
Artist
page 129

Debbie Fleming Caffery (b. 1948)
Sleeping Lizards, 1986, black and white silver print, 24"x 20," Courtesy of the Artist
page 150

Patty Carroll (b. 1946)
Sun Studio, Memphis, 1994, ekta print, 24" x 20," Courtesy of the Artist
page 106

Henri Cartier-Bresson (b. 1908)
Mississippi, 1962, gelatin silver print, 10"x 15," Courtesy of Helen Wright, The
Atelier Group, Ltd. and Magnum Photos, New York
Page 63

Tseng Kwong Chi (1950-1990)
Graceland, Tennessee, 1979, 1979, vintage gelatin silver print, 14 3/4"x15,"
Collection of Dr. James K. Patterson, MD, Memphis; Tseng Kwong Chi Estate and
Julie Saul Gallery, New York
Page 105

William Christenberry (b. 1936)
Church Across Field of Cotton, Pickinsville, Alabama, 1981, 1981, EK74 photograph, 9"x 13," © William Christenberry, Courtesy of Charlotte and Joel Bernsen,
Memphis
page 141

William Christenberry (b. 1936)
Abandoned House in Field Near Montgomery, Alabama, 1971, 1971, EK74 photograph, 3 1/8" x 4 7/8," © William Christenberry, Courtesy of Lisa Kurts Gallery,
Memphis
page 28

William Christenberry (b. 1936)
From The Klan Room, 1982, 1982, EK74 photograph, 20"x14 1/4," ©
William Christenberry, Courtesy of Dr. James K. Patterson, MD, Memphis
page 91

William Christenberry (b. 1936)
Window of Palmist Building, Havana Junction, Alabama ,1981, 1981,
EK74 photograph, 17 1/2"x 22," ©William Christenberry, Courtesy of
Charlotte and Joel Bernsen, Memphis
page 49

William Christenberry (b. 1936)
Grave with Bed as Marker, Near Faunsdale, Alabama, 1965, 1965, EK74
photograph, 3 1/4"x 4 3/4," ©William Christenberry, Courtesy of Lisa
Kurts Gallery, Memphis
Not Illustrated

Maude Schuyler Clay (b. 1953)
*To the Memory of Emmett Till, Cassidy Bayou, Sumner, Tallahatchie County,
Mississippi, 1998,* 1998, fiber-base, sepia-toned silver gelatin print,
14"x18," Courtesy of the Artist and Ariel Meyerowitz Gallery, New York
page 39

Florestine Perrault Collins (1895 - 1988)
Mae Fuller Keller, n.d, gelatin silver print, hand painted, 10"x 8," Courtesy
of Arthe' A. Anthony
page 65

Ralston Crawford (1906 - 1978)
Luzianne Coffee Can on Wall Vault, c.1950-1960, gelatin silver print,
6 1/2"x 91/2," Ralston Crawford/The Historic New Orleans Collection,
1983.33.11
page 116

Ralston Crawford (1906 - 1978)
New Orleans, 1961, "The Second Line (really jumping)", gelatin silver print,
8 1/2"x 13 1/2," Courtesy of Laurence Miller Gallery, New York
page 124

Ralston Crawford (1906 - 1978)
Iron Fence, New Orleans, 1959, vintage gelatin, silver print mounted to
board, 16 5/8"x 11 1/8," Courtesy of Laurence Miller Gallery, New York
page 5

Jack Delano (b. 1914)
Convicts in the County Jail. Greene County, Georgia, June, 1941, gelatin
silver print, printed later, Edition #4/25, 9"x 9," Courtesy of Howard
Greenberg Gallery, New York
page 85

Lee Friedlander (b. 1934)
Memphis, TN, 1973, 1973, gelatin silver print, 7 3/8"x 11 1/8," Lee Friedlander
Courtesy of Janet Borden Gallery, New York
page 122

Lee Friedlander (b. 1934)
New Orleans, 1970, 1970, gelatin silver print,13"x 8 1/2," Lee Friedlander
Courtesy of Janet Borden Gallery, New York
page 81

William Greiner (b. 1957)
Color T.V. in Bayou, 1993, c-print (color photograph), 20"x 24," Courtesy of the
Artist
page 146

Whit Griffin (b. 1980)
Recluse, 1999, 35mm photograph,10"x 8," Courtesy of the Artist
page 117

Lewis Wickes Hine (1874-1940)
Girls at Work in Textile Mill, from "Child Labor (Textiles) series," c.1912, gelatin silver print, printed later, 5"x 6 3/4," Collection of the George Eastman House, International Museum of Photography and Film, Rochester, NY
Page 111

Birney Imes (b. 1951)
Bell's Place, 1984, type "c"print, 20"x 24," © Birney Imes, Courtesy Bonni Benrubi Gallery, New York
page 101

Birney Imes (b. 1951)
Turk's Place, Leflore County, 1989, 1989, type "c"print, 20" x 24," © Birney Imes, Courtesy Bonni Benrubi Gallery, New York
page 57

Birney Imes (b. 1951)
Bailey's Late Nite Spot, Rolling Fork, MS, 1984, color photograph, 18" x 22 1/2," Collection of The Ogden Museum of Southern Art, New Orleans
Page 144

Dorothea Lange (1895 - 1965)
Lunchtime for Cotton Hoers, Mississippi Delta, June 1937, fiber base print, printed later, 10 1/2"x 10 1/8," Collection of the Library of Congress, Prints and Photographs Division, Farm Security Administration-Office of War Information Photograph Collection, [LC-USF34-017456-E]
page 42

Dorothea Lange (1895 - 1965)
Cotton Picker, Eutaw, Alabama, c. 1939, silver gelatin print, 5 1/4"x 9," Private Collection
page 45

Clarence John Laughlin (1905 - 1985)
Do Not Be Possessed By Dreams of Glory #2, 1948, c-print, 12 3/4"x 10,"
By Clarence John Laughlin/© The Historic New Orleans Collection, 1987.20.16
Not Illustrated

Clarence John Laughlin (1905 - 1985)
Elegy for the Old South #2, 1941, mixed media,10"x 13 1/2," By Clarence John Laughlin/© The Historic New Orleans Collection, 1987.247.2.57
page 4

Clarence John Laughlin (1905 - 1985)
Magnificent Avenue, Number One, 1947, gelatin silver print, 10 1/4"x 13 1/4," By Clarence John Laughlin/© The Historic New Orleans Collection, 1987.247.1.941
page 27

Clarence John Laughlin (1905 - 1985)
Elegy for Moss Land, 1940, gelatin silver print,10 1/2"x 13 1/2," By Clarence John Laughlin/© The Historic New Orleans Collection, 1987.247.1.888
page 33

David Julian Leonard (b. 1962)
*Payne's Bar B Q,*1995, chromogenic print, 12 5/8"x19 1/4," Courtesy of the Artist
page 87

David Julian Leonard (b. 1962)
Untitled (Feathers and Confederate Flag), 1995, chromogenic print, 13 x 19 1/2," Courtesy of the Artist.
Not Illustrated

David Julian Leonard (b. 1962)
Elephant's Graveyard, 1996, chromogenic print, 14 3/4"x 22," Courtesy of the Artist
page 46

David Julian Leonard (b. 1962)
Hunt & Fish & Fireworks for Jesus, 2000, chromogenic print, 14 1/4"x 21," Courtesy of the Artist.
page 143

C.C. Lockwood (b. 1949)
Flat Lake Sunset, 1980, cibachrome print, artist's proof, 19 1/2" x 13," Collection of The Ogden Museum of Southern Art, New Orleans
page 151

Peter Sekaer (1901 - 1950)
Irish Channel, Future Site of St. Thomas Housing Project, St. Thomas and Felicity Streets, New Orleans, c. 1938, vintage gelatin silver print, 9"x 13," ©Peter Sekaer Estate, Courtesy of Howard Greenberg Gallery, New York
Not Illustrated

Peter Sekaer (1901 - 1950)
Phrenology, c. 1939, gelatin silver print, 8"X 6 1/4," By Peter Sekaer/The Historic New Orleans Collection, 1981.311.5, © Peter Sekaer Estate, Courtesy of Howard Greenberg Gallery, New York
Page 92

Peter Sekaer (1901 - 1950)
Zula Parade, Float with Maskers, c. 1939, gelatin silver print, 6 1/4" X 6," By Peter Sekaer/The Historic New Orleans Collection, 1981, 311.10, ©Peter Sekaer Estate, Courtesy of Howard Greenberg Gallery, New York
Page 1

Peter Sekaer (1901 - 1950)
Mardi Gras Audience, c. 1939, gelatin silver print, 4 1/4"x 7," By Peter Sekaer/The Historic New Orleans Collection, 1981.311.7, ©Peter Sekaer Estate, Courtesy of Howard Greenberg Gallery, New York
page 115

Andres Serrano (b. 1950)
Klanswoman (Grand Klaliff II), 1990, cibachrome, silicone, plexiglass, wood frame, 60" x 49," Courtesy of Paula Cooper, New York
Page 108

Mike Smith (b. 1951)
Cash Hollow, TN, 1999, ekta color print, 20" x 24," Courtesy of Yancey Richardson Gallery, New York
Page 119

W. Eugene Smith (1919 - 1978)
KKK Grandmother, c. 1951 -58, silver print, 8" x 6," Courtesy of Robert Mann Gallery, New York
Page 142

Jack Spencer (b. 1951)
Happy Child, Como, Mississippi, 1996, 1996, photograph, 20" x 23," Courtesy of the Artist
Page 93

Jack Spencer (b. 1951)
Sheldon Church Ruins (burned by General Sherman 1865), Sheldon, South Carolina, 1998, 1998, photograph, 20" x 23 7/8," Courtesy of the Artist
Page 40

Mark Steinmetz (b. 1961)
New Orleans, 1995, 1995, gelatin silver print, 16"x 20," Courtesy of Yancey Richardson Gallery, New York
Page 100

Mark Steinmetz (b. 1961)
Athens, Georgia, 1996, 1996, gelatin silver print, 16" x 20," Courtesy of Yancey Richardson Gallery, New York
Page 69

Guenevere Taft (b. 1972)
"Liquor Store Series, Off of I-40, West Memphis, Arkansas," 1999, c-print, 6" x 6", Courtesy of the Artist and David Thompson, FRNKNDZN
Page 88

Doris Ulmann (1882 - 1934)
#350, n.d. photo adhered to mat, 8" x 6", Negative #70264, The Doris Ulmann Collection, © Collection of The New -York Historical Society
page 41

Doris Ulmann (1882 - 1934)
Mr. Rithcie, Viper, KY, c. 1933, gelatin silver print, 8" x 6," Courtesy of Howard Greenberg Gallery, New York
Page 82

Jeane Umbreit (b. 1953)
In Observance of Front Porch Etiquette, 1988, gelatin silver print, hand-colored, 10" x 8," Courtesy of David Lusk Gallery, Memphis
Page 120

Jeane Umbreit (b. 1953)
Cotton Exchange, 1988, gelatin silver print, hand-colored, 11" x 14," Courtesy of David Lusk Gallery, Memphis
page 149

James Perry Walker (b. 1945)
Gathering Eggs, 1979, selenium-toned silver print, 16" x 20," Courtesy of the Artist
Page 61

Eudora Welty (b. 1909)
Grenada County, 1930's, silver paper, toned, edition #163/300, from the series "Home Places, 5 Photographs by Eudora Welty," 11" x 6," Courtesy of William and Cheryl Bearden, Memphis © Eudora Welty Collection, Mississippi, Department of Archives and History, 1997
Page 31

Eudora Welty (b. 1909)
Storekeeper, Rankin County, Mississippi. c. 1935, toned gelatin silver print, printed later, Edition #46/60, 17 1/4" x 12 5/8," from "The Eudora Welty Portfolio," Mississippi Department of Archives and History, Diogenes Editions, Courtesy of Howard Greenberg Gallery, New York, ©Eudora Welty Collection, Mississippi Department of Archives and History, 1992
Page 32

Eudora Welty (b. 1909)
Saturday Strollers, Grenada, 1935, silver paper, toned,17 3/8" x 10," Edition #47/60, "The Eudora Welty Portfolio," Diogenes Editions in cooperation with the Mississippi Department of Archives and History, Collection of Logan Young, Memphis, ©Eudora Welty Collection, Mississippi Department of Archives and History, 1992
Page 96

Eudora Welty (b. 1909)
Bird Pageant Jackson, 1930's, silver paper, toned, 17 3/8" x 10," Edition #47/60, "The Eudora Welty Portfolio," Diogenes Editions in cooperation with the Mississippi Department of Archives and History, Collection of Logan Young, Memphis, ©Eudora Welty Collection, Mississippi Department of Archives and History, 1992, Courtesy of Logan Young
Not Illustrated

Edward Weston (1886 - 1958)
On Route U.S. 61, Mississippi, 1941, gelatin silver print, 7 1/2" x 9 1/2," Collection of The Royal Photographic Society, Bath, UK, ©1981 Center for Creative Photography, Arizona Board of Regents
Page 71

Ernest Withers (b. 1922)
Boarding House Bathroom from which James Earl Ray Shot Dr. King, 422 South Main Street, Memphis, April, *1968,* black and white photograph, 16" x 15," Courtesy of the Artist
Page 73

Ernest Withers (b. 1922)
National Guard Helicopter and Troops Prepare to Take James Meredith to University of Mississippi from Millington Naval Base, 1963, black and white photograph, 15 3/8" x 15 3/8," Courtesy of the Artist
Not Illustrated

Ernest Withers (b. 1922)
Destruction on Beale Street, Memphis, After the Sanitation Workers' March, March 1968, black and white photograph, 15" x 18," Courtesy of the Artist
Page 90

Marion Post Wolcott (1910 - 1990)
Gambling with Their "Cotton Money" in Back of a Juke Joint, Clarksdale, Mississippi, 1939, gelatin silver print, 11" x 14," Courtesy of Yancey Richardson Gallery, New York
Page 113

Marion Post Wolcott (1910 - 1990)
Negroes Jitterbugging in a Juke Joint, Clarksdale, Mississippi, 1939, gelatin silver print, 14" x 11," Courtesy of Yancey Richardson Gallery, New York
Page 114

Marion Post Wolcott (1910 - 1990)
Board and Split Rail Fences Around Fields of Shocked Corn. Near Marion, Virginia, 1940, gelatin silver print, 11" x 14," Courtesy of Yancey Richardson Gallery, New York
Page 148

Marion Post Wolcott (1910 - 1990)
Resting from Hoeing Cotton, on the Allen Plantation, a F S A Cooperative, Natchitoches, Louisiana, 1940, gelatin silver print, 14" x 11," Courtesy of Yancey Richardson Gallery, New York
Page 30

Logan Young
Untitled, 1999, 11" x 14," black and white photograph, Courtesy of the Artist
Page 152

Logan Young
Untitled, 1999, 14" x 10 3/4," Courtesy of the Artist
Not Illustrated